Educational Vouchers:
Concepts and Controversies

Educational Vouchers: Concepts and Controversies

Edited by
GEORGE R. La NOUE
Teachers College, Columbia University

Teachers College Press
Teachers College, Columbia University
New York and London

© 1972 by Teachers College, Columbia University
Library of Congress Catalog Card Number: 78-187726

Manufactured in the United States of America

George R. La Noue

Introduction

Few concepts have ever raised simultaneously as many hopes and fears about the future of American education as has the idea of educational vouchers. Voucher proponents want to change the traditional system of using tax funds to finance public schools to an arrangement of providing tax vouchers to individual parents, who would purchase education in a marketplace of diverse schools. There is no single voucher proposal. Some advocate vouchers that would be highly regulated to avoid discrimination and inequality, whereas others urge unregulated vouchers that would encourage the maximum variety of educational alternatives. Similarly, compensatory vouchers that provide additional amounts for poor families are supported by some, whereas others insist all families should receive equal amounts. Debate over the probable impact of the various types of vouchers on educational quality and equality has led to a fierce controversy. The purpose of this volume is to juxtapose the perspectives and the arguments being used in the debate, so that the reader can make his own policy judgments.

As the articles in Part I illustrate, vouchers are not a new concept, either intellectually or legislatively. Not much attention was paid to the idea by the federal government, however, until the Nixon administration. Democratic presidents supported programs with some of the characteristics of vouchers, like the G. I. Bill educational grants and college scholarships, but these programs were not viewed as challenging or restructuring public education. Most federal educational dollars have gone directly to governmental units or to the schools themselves.

Voucher advocates within the Nixon administration come from several sources. The economic theory in Milton Friedman's essay in Part I represents a traditional Republican philosophy of the marketplace, so vouchers have ideological support in the party. As Kevin Phillips suggests in his book, vouchers may also have some political utility for the party. Public support of private schools, he maintains, might unite ethnic constituencies in the North with white segregationists in the South to produce *The Emerging Republican Majority*. The development of actual voucher plans, however, has come from a less predictable source, the Office of Economic Opportunity. Since its mission has been redefined by President Nixon from that of a large-scale funder of community action programs to that of a smaller budget experimenter with social reform, OEO has come to support vouchers. Its rationale is that neither the massive infusions of federal funds nor the attempts at integration have improved education for minority group students. Many persons who are unsympathetic to *laissez faire* economics or Republican election strategies share OEO's conclusion about the need for radical reform of public education.

In this group certainly would be Christopher Jencks, the former education editor of *The New Republic* and now a professor of education at Harvard University. It was to Jencks and the Center for the Study of Public Policy at Harvard that OEO turned to develop a voucher plan that would benefit poor and minority groups. In a 220-page report issued in March 1970 and summarized in his articles in Part II, Jencks analyzes several kinds of vouchers. Although he supports a voucher that is carefully regulated and provides additional funds for poor children, he warns that a voucher system without these features "could be the most serious setback for the education of disadvantaged children in the history of the United States." Recognizing this dilemma, the principal debate among the authors in Part III is over the possibility of implementing an ideal voucher program without creating the risks of uncontrolled or anti-social vouchers.

After the Jencks report, John E. Coons, William H. Clune III, and Stephen D. Sugarman published *Private Wealth and Public Education*. Their position, summarized in a selection in Part II, supports another voucher plan that would equalize educational resources among school districts and at the same time permit a family to choose different levels of school quality. The Office of Economic Opportunity has decided to adopt the basic Jencks recommendations and to seek the cooperation of local school systems to launch several 5- to 8-year voucher experiments. Discussions were held with officials in many cities, but the idea proved difficult to sell. In at least three cities—Minneapolis, Kansas City, and Milwaukee—the proposal to participate in a voucher experiment was turned down by the school boards after public hearings. In February 1971, however, OEO announced that it had awarded planning grants to school authorities in Gary, Indiana; Alum Rock, California; and Seattle, Washington.

In the meantime, a formidable coalition opposed to vouchers began to mobilize. Indeed, there is a certain irony in the fact that Richard Nixon's support of vouchers has resuscitated the anti-private school aid coalition that Lyndon Johnson so skillfully divided and conquered as he maneuvered to pass the Elementary and Secondary Education Act in 1965. The whole public school establishment (the National Education Association, the American Federation of Teachers, the American Association of School Administrators, the National School Boards Association, and the National Congress of Parents and Teachers), as well as religious groups (the Baptist Joint Committee and the American Jewish Congress) and secular organizations (the American Civil Liberties

Union), are now formally opposed to vouchers. This coalition was successful in pressuring Congressional Committees into holding hearings on vouchers (see Part IV), but it was not able to obtain legislative prohibition of OEO's proposal. Although vouchers mustered little outright enthusiasm on Capitol Hill, few Congressmen wanted to kill something called an experiment. Given the controversy vouchers have created and OEO's uncertain future, however, whether its voucher plans will ever be fully implemented cannot now be determined.

Even if the federal voucher plan does not eventually survive its opposition, vouchers will be adopted by some states and, perhaps, even by some local communities. After *Brown v. Board of Education* (1954), several Southern states enacted voucher programs to avoid desegregation, but the federal courts, as illustrated in *Poindexter v. Louisiana* (1967), reprinted in Part I, overturned those laws. Several other recent court decisions, however, may have inadvertently increased the popularity of vouchers by threatening the core of public school support in white, middle-class suburbs. In *Serrano v. Priest* (1971), the California Supreme Court, followed by federal court decisions in Minnesota and Texas, ruled that dependence on local property taxes resulted in unconstitutional fiscal inequities among school districts and that some other financing system must be found. At about the same time, federal courts in Detroit and Richmond suggested that school segregation resulting from housing patterns and site selection patterns must be remedied and that may require cross-busing throughout entire metropolitan areas. If these legal trends are affirmed, suburban parents may find that local public schools, stripped of their fiscal advantages and homogenous student bodies, are not as attractive as private schools. Among private schools, however, the largest system (Catholic) has been shrinking steadily for the last six years and other systems are increasingly expensive. Furthermore, the Supreme Court in *Lemon v. Kurtzman* (1971) ruled that the direct approaches states had developed for aiding private schools are unconstitutional "entanglements" of church and state.

Consequently, most observers believe that the only way left to provide substantial aid to private schools is through vouchers. Since regulated vouchers might also create an entanglement between state and church schools, attention is increasingly focused on unregulated vouchers or tax credits. A state or federal income tax credit for private schooling would have the same functional consequences as a voucher. Only the collecting and payment mechanisms are different. It is widely believed that the White House Panel on Non-Public Education will recommend some form of tax credit when it reports in March 1972. In the meantime, Maryland and Pennsylvania have passed partially compensatory but non-regulated voucher systems in order to stabilize their parochial school enrollments, and California, Colorado, Illinois, Ohio, and New York are considering such legislation. Hawaii and Minnesota have adopted the tax credit approach. In a June 1969 Gallup Poll, 59% of the respondents said that if a voucher plan were available they would send their children to private or parochial schools. It is possible that problems in public schools and reactions to the recent federal court decisions on finance and busing have increased that percentage.

The voucher concept then is very much alive, but there are several major obstacles to implementing it at state and local levels. If voucher legislation includes parochial schools it will surely contravene many state constitutions. If it eliminates parochial schools, it will lose essential political support, since in most states most private schools are religiously sponsored. Aside from constitutional barriers, there are reams of state laws and regulations that might inhibit the operation of schools through state-funded voucher programs. Finally, since the major teacher and school administrator organizations are against vouchers, their political power and contract provisions may bar vouchers.

Nevertheless, despite these obstacles, voucher and tax credit plans have been and will continue to be implemented. Although there are many voucher approaches, all vouchers restructure the triangular relationship among parents, schools, and governments. Consequently, they raise the most fundamental kinds of issues about the future of American education. Some questions to keep in mind while reading this book are listed below.

1. Educational systems can be evaluated normatively or empirically by using absolute or comparative standards. As you evaluate American schools, what is really wrong and what are the priorities of things to be changed?

2. How do the assets and liabilities of vouchers compare with such other proposals for educational reform as parent participation through school decentralization, new accountability systems, performance contracting, shared time, and purchase of services?

3. What ought to be the relative educational rights and responsibilities of students, parents, teachers, and society? How does the equation change with the level of education (i.e., elementary vs. secondary)? How does the equation change with the degree to which education is tax financed?

4. Should the state use its educational resources to overcome or encourage differences among social groups? Does your answer depend on whether the group is ethnic, racial, religious, class, or sexual?

5. Are there any common values and experiences in the American culture that all children should share through schools? When does educational pluralism become a segregation or multiple indoctrination system? Do vouchers create an irreconcilable conflict between diversity and equality?

6. Should vouchers be relatively regulated or unregulated? What level of government should decide? Who should enforce the decision?

7. Would the marketplace be a sufficient regulator? What are real effects of marketplace competition in contemporary American society? Are the educational marketplace and product similar enough to economic sectors to make comparisons?

Contents

PART I

The Unregulated Voucher

On Liberty

In this portion of his classic work *On Liberty*
(1859), John Stuart Mill strives to prove that,
contrary to sentiment in mid-Victorian
England, education is a societal responsibility.
His desire to reconcile that premise with
his generally libertarian attitude against
government intervention led him to suggest an
educational voucher system. He believed
this arrangement could assist poor families
without creating the justification for state
control of the curriculum. The relationship of
the government to private schools has been
a continuing controversy in England as in this
country. Marjorie Cruickshanks' book,
Church and State in English Education (1963),
provides an historical description; a
contemporary appraisal of the English
"solution" can be found in Stafford Clayton's
Religion and Schooling: *A Comparative
Study* (1969).

... It is in the case of children that misapplied notions of liberty are a real obstacle to the fulfillment by the State of its duties. One would almost think that a man's children were supposed to be literally, and not metaphorically, a part of himself, so jealous is opinion of the smallest interference of law with his absolute and exclusive control over them, more jealous than of almost any interference with his own freedom of action: so much less do the generality of mankind value liberty than power. Consider, for example, the case of education. Is it not almost a self-evident axiom that the State should require and compel the education, up to a certain standard, of every human being who is born its citizen? Yet who is there that is not afraid to recognize and assert this truth? Hardly anyone, indeed, will deny that it is one of the most sacred duties of the parents (or, as law and usage now stand, the father), after summoning a human being into the world, to give to that being an education fitting him to perform his part well in life toward others and toward himself. But while this is unanimously declared to be the father's duty, scarcely anybody, in this country, will bear to hear of obliging him to perform it. Instead of his being required to make any exertion or sacrifice for securing education to his child, it is left to his choice to accept it or not when it is provided gratis! It still remains unrecognized that to bring a child into existence without a fair prospect of being able, not only to provide food for its body, but instruction and training for its mind is a moral crime, both against the unfortunate offspring and against society; and that if the parent does not fulfill this obligation, the State ought to see it fulfilled at the charge, as far as possible, of the parent.

Were the duty of enforcing universal education once admitted there would be an end to the difficulties about what the State should teach, and how it should teach, which now convert the subject into a mere battlefield for sects and parties, causing the time and labor which should have been spent in educating to be wasted in quarreling about education. If the government would make up its mind to require for every child a good education, it might save itself the trouble of providing one. It might leave to parents to obtain the education where and how they pleased, and content itself with helping to pay the school fees of the poorer classes of children, and defraying the entire school expenses of those who have no one else to pay for them. The objections which are urged with reason against State education do not apply to the enforcement of education by the State, but to the State's taking upon itself to direct that education; which is a totally different thing. That the whole or any large part of the education of the people should be in State hands, I go as far as anyone in deprecating. All that has been said of the importance of individuality of character, and diversity in opinions and modes of conduct, involves, as of the same unspeakable importance, diversity of education. A general State education is a mere contrivance for molding people to be exactly like one another; and as the mold in which it casts them is that which pleases the predominant power in the government—whether this be a monarch, a priesthood, an aristocracy, or the majority of the existing generation—in proportion as it is efficient and successful, it establishes a despotism over the mind, leading by natural tendency to one over the body. An education established and controlled by the State should only exist, if it exist at all, as one among many competing experiments, carried on for the purpose of example and stimulus to keep the others up to a certain standard of excellence. Unless, indeed, when society in general is in so backward a state that it could not or would not provide for itself any proper institutions of education unless the government undertook the task, then, indeed, the government may, as the less of two great evils, take upon itself the business of schools and universities, as it may that of joint stock companies when private enterprise in a shape fitted for undertaking great works of industry does not exist in the country. But in general, if the country contains a sufficient number of persons qualified to provide education under government auspices, the same persons would be able and willing to give an equally good education on the voluntary principle, under the assurance of remuneration afforded by a law rendering education compulsory, combined with State aid to those unable to defray the expense.

The instrument for enforcing the law could be no other than public examinations, extending to all children and beginning at an early age. An age might be fixed at which every child must be examined, to ascertain if he (or she) is able to read. If a child proves unable, the father, unless he has some sufficient ground of excuse, might be subjected to a moderate fine, to be worked out, if necessary, by his labor, and the child might be put to school at his expense. Once in every year the examination should be renewed, with a gradually extending range of subjects, so as to make the universal acquisition and, what is more, retention of a certain minimum of general knowledge virtually compulsory. Beyond that minimum there should be voluntary examinations of all subjects, at which all who come up to a certain standard of proficiency might claim a certificate. To prevent the State from exercising, through these arrangements, an improper influence over opinion, the knowledge required for passing an examination (beyond the merely instrumental parts of knowledge, such as languages and their use) should, even in the higher classes of examinations, be confined to facts and positive science exclusively. The examinations on religion, politics, or other disputed topics should not turn on the truth or falsehood of opinions, but on the matter of fact that such and such an opinion is held, on such grounds, by such authors, or schools, or churches. Under this system, the rising generation would be no worse off in regard to all disputed truths than they are at present; they would be brought up either churchmen or dissenters as they now are, the State merely taking care that they should be instructed churchmen, or instructed dissenters. There would be nothing to hinder them from being taught religion, if their parents chose, at the same schools where they were taught other things. All attempts by the State to bias the conclusions of its citizens on disputed subjects are evil; but it may very properly offer to ascertain and certify that a person possesses the knowledge requisite to make his conclusions on any given subject worth attending to. A student of philosophy would be the better for being able to stand an examination both in Locke and in Kant, whichever of the two he takes up with, or even if with neither: and there is no reasonable objection to examining an atheist in the evidences of Christianity, provided he is not required to profess a belief in them. The examinations, however, in the higher branches of knowledge should, I conceive, be entirely voluntary. It would be giving too dangerous a power to governments were they allowed to exclude anyone from professions, even from the profession of teacher, for alleged deficiency of qualifications; and I think, with Wilhelm von Humboldt, that degrees or other public certificates of scientific or professional acquirements should be given to all who present themselves for examination and stand the test, but that such certificates should confer no advantage over competitors other than the weight which may be attached to their testimony by public opinion.

It is not in the matter of education only that misplaced notions of liberty prevent moral obligations on the part of parents from being recognized, and legal obligations from being imposed, where there are the strongest grounds for the former always, and in many cases for the latter also. The fact itself, of causing the existence of a human being, is one of the most responsible actions in the range of human life. To undertake this responsibility—to bestow a life which may be either a curse or a blessing—unless the being on whom it is to be bestowed will have at least the ordinary chances of a desirable existence, is a crime against that being. And in a country, either overpeopled or threatened with being so, to produce children, beyond a very small number, with the effect of reducing the reward of labor by their competition is a serious offense against all who live by the remuneration of their labor. The laws which, in many countries on the Continent, forbid marriage unless the parties can show that they have the means of supporting a family do not exceed the legitimate powers of the State; and whether such laws be expedient or not (a question mainly dependent on local circumstances and feelings), they are not objectionable as violations of liberty. Such laws are interferences of the State to prohibit a mischievous act—an act injurious to others, which ought to be a subject of reprobation and social stigma, even when it is not deemed expedient to superadd legal punishment. Yet the current ideas of liberty, which bend so easily to real infringements of the freedom of the individual in things which concern only himself, would repel the attempt to put any restraint upon his inclinations when the consequence of their indulgence is a life or lives of wretchedness and depravity to the offspring, with manifold evils to those sufficiently within reach to be in any way affected by their actions. When we compare the strange respect of mankind for liberty with their strange want of respect for it, we might imagine that a man had an indispensable right to do harm to others, and no right at all to please himself without giving pain to anyone.

The Role of Government in Education

Milton Friedman's *Capitalism and Freedom* has been the major popular expression of virtues of classical marketplace theory in recent years. In this book, Friedman criticizes the government's role in redistributing resources and providing services like social security, parks, libraries, and, of course, schools. Professor Friedman, a University of Chicago economist, served as a consultant in Barry Goldwater's presidential campaign and has been the theorist behind several Nixon Administration programs, including welfare reform as well as vouchers.

Milton Friedman, Capitalism and Freedom *(Chicago: University of Chicago Press, 1962), pp.* 85-98.

Milton Friedman

Formal schooling is today paid for and almost entirely administered by government bodies or non-profit institutions. This situation has developed gradually and is now taken so much for granted that little explicit attention is any longer directed to the reasons for the special treatment of schooling even in countries that are predominantly free enterprise in organization and philosophy. The result has been an indiscriminate extension of governmental responsibility.

In terms of the principles developed in chapter ii, governmental intervention into education can be rationalized on two grounds. The first is the existence of substantial "neighborhood effects," i.e., circumstances under which the action of one individual imposes significant costs on other individuals for which it is not feasible to make him compensate them, or yields significant gains to other individuals for which it is not feasible to make them compensate him—circumstances that make voluntary exchange impossible. The second is the paternalistic concern for children and other irresponsible individuals. Neighborhood effects and paternalism have very different implications for (1) general education for citizenship, and (2) specialized vocational education. The grounds for governmental intervention are widely different in these two areas and justify very different types of action.

One further preliminary remark: it is important to distinguish between "schooling" and "education." Not all schooling is education nor all education, schooling. The proper subject of concern is education. The activities of government are mostly limited to schooling.

General Education for Citizenship   A stable and democratic society is impossible without a minimum degree of literacy and knowledge on the part of most citizens and without widespread acceptance of some common set of values. Education can contribute to both. In consequence, the gain from the education of a child accrues not only to the child or to his parents but also to other members of the society. The education of my child contributes to your welfare by promoting a stable and democratic society. It is not feasible to identify the particular individuals (or families) benefited and so to charge for the services rendered. There is therefore a significant "neighborhood effect."

What kind of governmental action is justified by this particular neighborhood effect? The most obvious is to require that each child receive a minimum amount of schooling of a specified kind. Such a requirement could be imposed upon the parents without further government action, just as owners of buildings, and frequently of automobiles, are required to adhere to specified standards to protect the safety of others. There is, however, a difference between the two cases. Individuals who cannot pay the costs of meeting the standards required for buildings or automobiles can generally divest themselves of the property by selling it. The requirement can thus generally be enforced without government subsidy. The separation of a child from a parent who cannot pay for the minimum required schooling is clearly inconsistent with our reliance on the family as the basic social unit and our belief in the freedom of the individual. Moreover, it would be very likely to detract from his education for citizenship in a free society.

If the financial burden imposed by such a schooling requirement could readily be met by the great bulk of the families in a community, it might still be both feasible and desirable to require the parents to meet the cost directly. Extreme cases could be handled by special subsidy provisions for needy families. There are many areas in the United States today where these conditions are satisfied. In these areas, it would be highly desirable to impose the costs directly on the parents. This would eliminate the governmental machinery now required to collect tax funds from all residents during the whole of their lives and then pay it back mostly to the same people during the period when their children are in school. It would reduce the likelihood that governments would also administer schools, a matter discussed further below. It would increase the likelihood that the subsidy component of school expenditures would decline as the need of such subsidies declined with increasing general levels of income. If, as now, the government pays for all or most schooling, a rise in income simply leads to a still larger circular flow of funds through the tax mechanism, and an expansion in the role of the government. Finally, but by no means least, imposing the costs on the parents would tend to equalize the social and private costs of having children and so promote a better distribution of families by size.[1]

Differences among families in resources and in number of children, plus the

---

1 It is by no means so fantastic as may appear that such a step would noticeably affect the size of families. For example, one explanation of the lower birth rate among higher than among lower socio-economic groups may well be that children are relatively more expensive to the former, thanks in considerable measure to the higher standards of schooling they maintain, the costs of which they bear.

imposition of a standard of schooling involving very sizable costs, make such a policy hardly feasible in many parts of the United States. Both in such areas, and in areas where such a policy would be feasible, government has instead assumed the financial costs of providing schooling. It has paid, not only for the minimum amount of schooling required of all, but also for additional schooling at higher levels available to youngsters but not required of them. One argument for both steps is the "neighborhood effects" discussed above. The costs are paid because this is the only feasible means of enforcing the required minimum. Additional schooling is financed because other people benefit from the schooling of those of greater ability and interest, since this is a way of providing better social and political leadership. The gain from these measures must be balanced against the costs, and there can be much honest difference of judgment about how extensive a subsidy is justified. Most of us, however, would probably conclude that the gains are sufficiently important to justify some government subsidy.

These grounds justify government subsidy of only certain kinds of schooling. To anticipate, they do not justify subsidizing purely vocational training which increases the economic productivity of the student but does not train him for either citizenship or leadership. It is extremely difficult to draw a sharp line between the two types of schooling. Most general schooling adds to the economic value of the student—indeed it is only in modern times and in a few countries that literacy has ceased to have a marketable value. And much vocational training broadens the student's outlook. Yet the distinction is meaningful. Subsidizing the training of veterinarians, beauticians, dentists, and a host of other specialists, as is widely done in the United States in governmentally supported educational institutions, cannot be justified on the same grounds as subsidizing elementary schools or, at a higher level, liberal arts colleges. Whether it can be justified on quite different grounds will be discussed later in this chapter.

The qualitative argument from "neighborhood effects" does not, of course, determine the specific kinds of schooling that should be subsidized or by how much they should be subsidized. The social gain presumably is greatest for the lowest levels of schooling, where there is the nearest approach to unanimity about content, and declines continuously as the level of schooling rises. Even this statement cannot be taken completely for granted. Many governments subsidized universities long before they subsidized lower schools. What forms of education have the greatest social advantage and how much of the community's limited resources should be spent on them must be decided by the judgment of the community expressed through its accepted political channels. The aim of this analysis is not to decide these questions for the community but rather to clarify the issues involved in making a choice, in particular whether it is appropriate to make the choice on a communal rather than individual basis.

As we have seen, both the imposition of a minimum required level of schooling and the financing of this schooling by the state can be justified by the "neighborhood effects" of schooling. A third step, namely the actual administration of educational institutions by the government, the "nationalization," as it were, of the bulk of the "education industry" is much more difficult to justify on these, or, so far as I can see, any other, grounds. The desirability of such nationalization has seldom been faced explicitly. Governments have, in the main, financed schooling by paying directly the costs of running educational institutions. Thus this step seemed required by the decision to subsidize schooling. Yet the two steps could readily be separated. Governments could require a minimum level of schooling financed by giving parents vouchers redeemable for a specified maximum sum per child per year if spent on "approved" educational services. Parents would then be free to spend this sum and any additional sum they themselves provided on purchasing educational services from an "approved" institution of their own choice. The educational services could be rendered by private enterprises operated for profit, or by non-profit institutions. The role of the government would be limited to insuring that the schools met certain minimum standards, such as the inclusion of a minimum common content in their programs, much as it now inspects restaurants to insure that they maintain minimum sanitary standards. An excellent example of a program of this sort is the United States educational program for veterans after World War II. Each veteran who qualified was given a maximum sum per year that could be spent at any institution of his choice, provided it met certain minimum standards. A more limited example is the provision in Britain whereby local authorities pay the fees of some students attending non-state schools. Another is the arrangement in France whereby the state pays part of the costs for students attending non-state schools.

One argument for nationalizing schools resting on a "neighborhood effect" is that it might otherwise be impossible to provide the common core of values deemed requisite for social stability. The imposition of minimum standards on privately conducted schools, as suggested above, might not be enough to achieve this result. The issue can be illustrated concretely in terms of schools run by different religious groups. Such schools, it can be argued, will instil sets of values that are inconsistent with one another and with those instilled in non-sectarian schools; in this way, they convert education into a divisive rather than a unifying force.

Carried to its extreme, this argument would call not only for governmentally administered schools, but also for compulsory attendance at such schools. Existing arrangements in the United States and most other Western countries are a halfway house. Governmentally administered schools are available but not compulsory. However, the link between the financing of schooling and its administration places other schools at a disadvantage; they get the benefit of little or none of the governmental funds spent on schooling—a situation that has been the source of much political dispute, particularly in France and at present in the United States. The elimination of this disadvantage might, it is feared, greatly strengthen the parochial schools and so render the problem of achieving a common core of values even more difficult.

Persuasive as this argument is, it is by no means clear that it is valid or that denationalizing schooling would have the effects suggested. On grounds of principle, it conflicts with the preservation of freedom itself. Drawing a line between providing for the common social values required for a stable society, on the one hand, and indoctrination inhibiting freedom of thought and belief, on the other is another of those vague boundaries that is easier to mention than to define.

In terms of effects, denationalizing schooling would widen the range of choice available to parents. If, as at present, parents can send their children to public schools without special payment, very few can or will send them to other schools unless they too are subsidized. Parochial schools are at a disadvantage in not getting any of the public funds devoted to schooling, but they have the compensating advantage of being run by institutions that are willing to subsidize them and can raise funds to do so. There are few other sources of subsidies for private schools. If present public expenditures on schooling were made available to parents regardless of where they send their children, a wide variety of schools would spring up to meet the demand. Parents could express their views about schools directly by withdrawing their children from one school and sending them to another, to a much greater extent than is now possible. In general, they can now take this step only at considerable cost—by sending their children to a private school or by changing their residence. For the rest, they can express their views only through cumbrous political channels. Perhaps a somewhat greater degree of freedom to choose schools could be made available in a governmentally administered system, but it would be difficult to carry this freedom very far in view of the obligation to provide every child with a place. Here, as in other fields, competitive enterprise is likely to be far more efficient in meeting consumer demand than either nationalized enterprises or enterprises run to serve other purposes. The final result may therefore be that parochial schools would decline rather than grow in importance.

A related factor working in the same direction is the understandable reluctance of parents who send their children to parochial schools to increase taxes to finance higher public school expenditures. As a result, those areas where parochial schools are important have great difficulty raising funds for public schools. Insofar as quality is related to expenditure, as to some extent it undoubtedly is, public schools tend to be of lower quality in such areas and hence parochial schools are relatively more attractive.

Another special case of the argument that governmentally conducted schools are necessary for education to be a unifying force is that private schools would tend to exacerbate class distinctions. Given greater freedom about where to send their children, parents of a kind would flock together and so prevent a healthy intermingling of children from decidedly different backgrounds. Whether or not this argument is valid in principle, it is not at all clear that the stated results would follow. Under present arrangements, stratification of residential areas effectively restricts the intermingling of children from decidedly different backgrounds. In addition, parents are not now prevented from sending their children to private schools. Only a highly limited class can or does do so, parochial schools aside, thus producing further stratification.

Indeed, this argument seems to me to point in almost the diametrically opposite direction—toward the denationalizing of schools. Ask yourself in what respect the inhabitant of a low income neighborhood, let alone of a Negro neighborhood in a large city, is most disadvantaged. If he attaches enough importance to, say, a new automobile, he can, by dint of saving, accumulate enough money to buy the same car as a resident of a high-income suburb. To do so, he need not move to that suburb. On the contrary, he can get the money partly by economizing on his living quarters. And this goes equally for clothes, or furniture, or books, or what not. But let a poor family in a slum have a gifted child and let it set such high value on his or her schooling that it is willing to scrimp and save for the purpose. Unless it can get special treatment, or scholarship assistance, at one of the very few private schools, the family is in a very difficult position. The "good" public schools are in the high income neighborhoods. The family might be willing to spend something in addition to what it pays in taxes to get better schooling for its child. But it can hardly afford simultaneously to move to the expensive neighborhood.

Our views in these respects are, I believe, still dominated by the small town which had but one school for the poor and rich residents alike. Under such circumstances, public schools may well have equalized opportunities. With the growth of urban and suburban areas, the situation has changed drastically. Our present school system, far from equalizing opportunity, very likely does the opposite. It makes it all the harder for the exceptional few—and it is they who are the hope of the future—to rise above the poverty of their initial state.

Another argument for nationalizing schooling is "technical monopoly." In small communities and rural areas, the number of children may be too small to justify more than one school of reasonable size, so that competition cannot be relied on to protect the interests of parents and children. As in other cases of technical monopoly, the alternatives are unrestricted private monopoly, state-controlled private monopoly, and public operation—a choice among evils. This argument, though clearly valid and significant, has been greatly weakened in recent decades by improvements in transportation and increasing concentration of the population in urban communities.

The arrangement that perhaps comes closest to being justified by these considerations—at least for primary and secondary education—is a combination of public and private schools. Parents who choose to send their children to private schools would be paid a sum equal to the estimated cost of educating a child in a public school, provided that at least this sum was spent on education in an approved school. This arrangement would meet the valid features of the "technical monopoly" argument. It would meet the just complaints of parents that if they send their children to private non-subsidized schools they are required to pay twice for education—once in the form of general taxes and once directly. It would permit competition to develop. The development and improvement of all schools would thus be stimulated. The injection of competition would do much to promote a healthy variety of schools. It would do much, also, to introduce flexibility into school systems. Not least of its benefits would be to make the salaries of school teachers responsive to market forces. It would thereby give public authorities an independent standard against which to judge salary scales and promote a more rapid adjustment to changes in conditions of demand and supply.

It is widely urged that the great need in schooling is more money to build more facilities and to pay higher salaries to teachers in order to attract better teachers. This seems a false diagnosis. The amount of money spent on schooling has been rising at an extraordinarily high rate, far faster than our total income. Teachers' salaries have been rising far faster than returns in comparable occupations. The problem is not primarily that we are spending too little money— though we may be—but that we are getting so little per dollar spent. Perhaps the amounts of money spent on magnificent structures and luxurious grounds at many schools are properly classified as expenditures on schooling. It is hard to accept them equally as expenditures on education. And this is equally clear with respect to courses in basket weaving, social dancing, and the numerous other special subjects that do such credit to the ingenuity of educators. I hasten to add that there can be no conceivable objection to parents' spending their own money on such frills if they wish. This is their business. The objection is to using money raised by taxation imposed on parents and non-parents alike for such purposes. Wherein are the "neighborhood effects" that justify such use of tax money?

A major reason for this kind of use of public money is the present system of combining the administration of schools with their financing. The parent who would prefer to see money used for better teachers and texts rather than coaches and corridors has no way of expressing this preference except by persuading a majority to change the mixture for all. This is a special case of the general principle that a market permits each to satisfy his own taste—effective proportional representation; whereas the political process imposes conformity. In addition, the parent who would like to spend some extra money on his child's education is greatly limited. He cannot add something to the amount now being spent to school his child and transfer his child to a correspondingly more costly school. If he does transfer his child, he must pay the whole cost and not simply the additional cost. He can only spend extra money easily on extra-curricular activities—dancing lessons, music lessons, etc. Since the private outlets for spending more money on schooling are so blocked, the pressure to spend more on the education of children manifests itself in ever higher public expenditures on items ever more tenuously related to the basic justification for governmental intervention into schooling.

As this analysis implies, the adoption of the suggested arrangements might well mean smaller governmental expenditures on schooling, yet higher total expenditures. It would enable parents to buy what they want more efficiently and thereby lead them to spend more than they now do directly and indirectly through taxation. It would prevent parents from being frustrated in spending more money on schooling by both the present need for conformity in how the money is spent and by the understandable reluctance on the part of persons not currently having children in school, and especially those who will not in the future have them in school, to impose higher taxes on themselves for purposes often far removed from education as they understand the term.[2]

With respect to teachers' salaries, the major problem is not that they are too low on the average—they may well be too high on the average—but that they are too uniform and rigid. Poor teachers are grossly overpaid and good teachers grossly underpaid. Salary schedules tend to be uniform and determined far more by seniority, degrees received, and teaching certificates acquired than by merit. This, too, is largely a result of the present system of governmental administration of schools and becomes more serious as the unit over which governmental control is exercised becomes larger. Indeed, this very fact is a major reason why professional educational organizations so strongly favor broadening the unit—from the local school district to the state, from the state to the federal government. In any bureaucratic, essentially civil-service organization, standard salary scales are almost inevitable; it is next to impossible to stimulate competition capable of providing wide differences in salaries according to merit. The educators, which means the teachers themselves, come to exercise primary control. The parent or local community comes to exercise little control. In any area, whether it be carpentry or plumbing or teaching, the majority of workers favor standard salary scales and oppose merit differentials, for the obvious reason

2 A striking example of the same effect in another field is the British National Health Service. In a careful and penetrating study, D. S. Lees establishes rather conclusively that, "Far from being extravagant, expenditure on NHS has been less than consumers would probably have chosen to spend in a free market. The record of hospital building in particular has been deplorable." "Health Through Choice," *Hobart Paper 14* (London: Institute of Economic Affairs, 1961), p. 58.

that the specially talented are always few. This is a special case of the general tendency for people to seek to collude to fix prices, whether through unions or industrial monopolies. But collusive agreements will generally be destroyed by competition unless the government enforces them, or at least renders them considerable support.

If one were to seek deliberately to devise a system of recruiting and paying teachers calculated to repel the imaginative and daring and self-confident and to attract the dull and mediocre and uninspiring, he could hardly do better than imitate the system of requiring teaching certificates and enforcing standard salary structures that has developed in the larger city and state-wide systems. It is perhaps surprising that the level of ability in elementary and secondary school teaching is as high as it is under these circumstances. The alternative system would resolve these problems and permit competition to be effective in rewarding merit and attracting ability to teaching.

Why has governmental intervention in schooling in the United States developed along the lines it has? I do not have the detailed knowledge of educational history that would be required to answer this question definitively. A few conjectures may nonetheless be useful to suggest the kinds of considerations that may alter the appropriate social policy. I am by no means sure that the arrangements I now propose would in fact have been desirable a century ago. Before the extensive growth in transportation, the "technical monopoly" argument was much stronger. Equally important, the major problem in the United States in the nineteenth and early twentieth century was not to promote diversity but to create the core of common values essential to a stable society. Great streams of immigrants were flooding the United States from all over the world, speaking different languages and observing diverse customs. The "melting pot" had to introduce some measure of conformity and loyalty to common values. The public school had an important function in this task, not least by imposing English as a common language. Under the alternative voucher scheme, the minimum standards imposed on schools to qualify for approval could have included the use of English. But it might well have been more difficult to insure that this requirement was imposed and satisfied in a private school system. I do not mean to conclude that the public school system was definitely preferable to the alternative, but only that a far stronger case could have been made for it then than now. Our problem today is not to enforce conformity; it is rather that we are threatened with an excess of conformity. Our problem is to foster diversity, and the alternative would do this far more effectively than a nationalized school system.

Another factor that may have been important a century ago was the combination of the general disrepute of cash grants to individuals ("handouts"), with the absence of an efficient administrative machinery to handle the distribution of vouchers and check their use. Such machinery is a phenomenon of modern times that has come to full flower with the enormous extension of personal taxation and of social security programs. In its absence, the administration of schools may have been regarded as the only possible way to finance education.

As some of the examples cited above (England and France) suggest, some features of the proposed arrangements are present in existing educational systems. And there has been strong and, I believe, increasing pressure for arrangements of this kind in most Western countries. This is perhaps partly explained by modern developments in governmental administrative machinery that facilitate such arrangements.

Although many administrative problems would arise in changing over from the present to the proposed system and in its administration, these seem neither insoluble nor unique. As in the denationalization of other activities, existing premises and equipment could be sold to private enterprises that wanted to enter the field. Thus, there would be no waste of capital in the transition. Since governmental units, at least in some areas, would continue to administer schools, the transition would be gradual and easy. The local administration of schooling in the United States and some other countries would similarly facilitate the transition, since it would encourage experimentation on a small scale. Difficulties would doubtless arise in determining eligibility for grants from a particular governmental unit, but this is identical with the existing problem of determining which unit is obligated to provide schooling facilities for a particular child. Differences in size of grants would make one area more attractive than another just as differences in the quality of schooling now have the same effect. The only additional complication is a possibly greater opportunity for abuse because of the greater freedom to decide where to educate children. Supposed difficulty of administration is a standard defense of the status quo against any proposed change; in this particular case, it is an even weaker defense than usual because existing arrangements must master not only the major problems raised by the proposed arrangements but also the additional problems raised by the administration of schools as a governmental function.

Freedom of Choice in Education

Although his role has been ignored by recent
voucher advocates, the major spokesman for
vouchers among conservative religious
constituencies has been Virgil C. Blum. Father
Blum, a Jesuit priest and professor of political
science at Marquette University, not only
has been a prolific writer but has founded
Citizens for Educational Freedom, which has
functioned in some states as a powerful
voucher lobby. In this piece from his book,
Freedom of Choice in Education (1958),
Father Blum sets out the precedents and
constructs the case for an unregulated voucher.

Virgil C. Blum, S.J., Freedom of Choice in Education *(New York: Macmillan, 1958), pp.
39-48.* © *1958 by Virgil C. Blum, S.J.*

Virgil C. Blum, S. J.

State governments are today subsidizing the education of only those children and students who attend state educational institutions, except for several states which give freedom of choice to scholarship winners. The education of each child in the public schools is subsidized, on the average, to the extent of about $400 a year. The education of each state university student is subsidized to the extent of roughly $1,300 a year, or more. But on the other hand, children and young men and women who attend independent educational institutions receive no educational subsidy whatsoever. The certificate and tax credit plans are methods by which government can subsidize their education, at least in part.

These plans raise no constitutional questions. The voucher plan provides that government make direct money grants in the form of vouchers or certificates to parents or guardians of all children attending approved independent schools. A voucher of $100, for example, would be valid when used in partial payment of tuition and signed by a parent or guardian and school principal. Under this plan government could also give vouchers of $500, for example, to college students to enable them to pay in part tuition and fees at independent institutions, or at government institutions in other than the student's state of residence. The plan is identical in principle with Federal money grants to veterans for the payment of tuition and fees in the schools of their choice, the well-known G.I. Bill.

The tax credit plan, on the other hand, provides that government give a tax offset to parents of all children attending approved independent tuition-charging schools. A tax credit of $100, for example, could be given to parents and guardians for each child attending an independent school for whom they pay tuition. In no case, however, would they get more than the tuition actually paid. Under this plan government could also give a tax credit of $500, for example, to parents or guardians, or to students themselves, to enable them to pay in part tuition and fees at independent institutions, or at government institutions in other than the student's state of residence.

Recent proposals for a tax credit for parents to enable them to send their children to the school of their choice do not provide for a lump-sum credit but rather a credit covering a certain per cent of the tuition and fees. The formula suggested by the Resolutions Committee of the Taxation Section of the American Bar Association at its 1954 convention, for example, "provides that 30 per cent of student tuition and fees actually paid by the taxpayer to the institution be applied as a tax credit on the amount of income tax otherwise payable." All tuition-paying taxpayers would receive the same tax benefits in dollars, regardless of whether they are in the 20 per cent, 50 per cent, or 91 per cent income tax bracket.

The tax deduction plan should be clearly distinguished from the tax credit plan. If the tuition is $800, for example, what tax benefits would the two plans give to parents who pay the tuition of their children? Under the tax deduction plan, the parent in the 20 per cent bracket would save $160 of taxes; if he is in the 50 per cent bracket he would save $400 of taxes. Under a tax credit plan providing for a 30 per cent credit on tuition and fees, on the other hand, the parent in the 20 per cent bracket and the parent in the 50 per cent bracket would be given equal tax relief. They would both be given a tax offset of $240 (30 per cent of $800). This amount would be subtracted from their personal tax bills.

Since the Federal Government does not operate a school system, it might well advance the national interest in education by extending a tax credit to all parents and students regardless of the school they attend.

From this analysis, it is clear that the voucher or tax credit plan involves no government aid to or support of church-related schools. The government subsidy is given directly to parents to enable them to pay in part their children's tuition at the school of their choice. Parents and their children alone are the beneficiaries of the subsidy.

The voucher or tax credit plan is designed to enable parents or students to pay a greater percentage of the cost of education. It does not propose to aid the school of the parent's or student's choice. The President's Committee on Education Beyond the High School observed, in discussing the G.I. Bill, that it "does not believe that this assistance to veterans was designed to help, even *indirectly*, the institutions. Actually it imposed an enormous burden on them, a burden they accepted as a part of their mission in our society, but a heavy financial and administrative burden nonetheless." When government helps parents and students pay *part* of a tuition which is itself considerably less than the cost of education at the school attended, no reasonable person would contend that government is subsidizing the school. The school, as the President's Committee pointed out, actually assumes an "enormous burden" in its efforts to promote the welfare of society. The school is not only not subsidized, but the school itself subsidizes the education of government-subsidized students.

It is fundamental that the state's educational obligations are not to *institutions;* its obligations are to *children.* Educational institutions are but *means* to help the state carry out its educational obligations. But in a pluralistic society one single school system cannot be an adequate means of education for all children since every school has religious and moral values. These values may be in conflict with the convictions of some children. The constitutional guarantees of freedom and equality require the state to make other educational provisions for these children.

This is simply to say that the state's obligations in education extend to each individual child and student. And these obligations must be fulfilled consistent with the child's rights and liberties under the Federal and state constitutions. In a totalitarian state, the government forces all children to accept the religious and moral values of the state schools. In a democracy, where freedom of thought and religion are protected by the Constitution, the government may not force children to accept the religious and moral values of the state schools.

A government may, indeed, establish a state school system. But since it cannot coerce attendance, constitutional guarantees demand that it seek other means to fulfill its educational obligations to children and students who, for philosophical or theological reasons, cannot conform to the established philosophical and theological values of state schools. This duty is incumbent on the state since it cannot demand the surrender of the constitutional right to attend an independent school or college as a condition for sharing in welfare benefits. The constitution compels the state to employ such means to secure a student's education as are not incompatible with his rights under the Constitution.

The voucher or tax credit plan enables the several states to fulfill their obligations to children and students in independent schools and colleges within the limits of existing constitutional provisions. The subsidy is given directly to parents. And parents, exercising freedom of choice, select the kind of education they want for their children in the open market of education. In this plan parents of children and students attending independent schools and colleges would pay tuition charges in part with government issued vouchers or tax credits. Thus the schools would in no way be subsidized with public funds, only parents and their children would be subsidized.

The voucher or tax credit plan is in principle the same as the plans the Federal Government adopted to enable veterans, war orphans, and the pages of Congress to get an education at the school of their choice. The direct subsidy principle, incorporating the principle of freedom of choice, was adopted, in one form or another, in the Servicemen's Readjustment Act of 1944, the Veterans' Readjustment Act of 1952, the War Orphans' Educational Assistance Act of 1956, and in the educational provisions of the Legislative Reorganization Act of 1946 for the education of the pageboys of Congress.

The Federal Government helped pay for the education of World War II veterans by paying the tuition and fees of the individual veteran at the school of his choice. The government, however, subsidized the education of Korean veterans by directly subsidizing the individual veteran to enable him to pay tuition and fees at the school of his choice. Today the government is subsidizing the education of war orphans by direct money grants to the individual student to enable him to pay tuition and fees at the school of his choice.

Individual veterans, with government subsidy in hand, paid tuition, fees, and incidental charges at one or other of our 481 nonsectarian, 474 Protestant, 265 Catholic, and 5 Jewish institutions of higher learning, or at one of our state colleges or universities. The college the veteran elected to attend not only received no government subsidy, but the college itself, since tuition does not fully cover actual educational costs, subsidized the veteran's education.

In this way the Federal Government has paid out many millions of dollars for the education of veterans in non-sectarian colleges and universities and in the colleges and universities of the several religious denominations. As a matter of fact, the government has spent millions of dollars for the education of no fewer than 36,000 veterans studying to become ministers of religion, most of them Protestants.

The beneficiaries of these expenditures, as we have seen, are the individual students; consequently, the constitutional question of separation of church and state cannot properly be raised. The principle that the state can subsidize the individual citizen without subsidizing the religion to which he adheres or the religious organizations to which he belongs has been repeatedly enunciated by the Supreme Court of the United States. A state may, for example, give textbooks to children attending church-related schools. "The schools," said the Court, "are not the beneficiaries of these appropriations. They obtain nothing from them, nor are they relieved of a single obligation, because of them. The school children and the state alone are the beneficiaries." A state may also subsidize parents to help them transport their children to the school of their choice, even though the school be church-related. When such grants are made to parents, declared the Court, "the State contributes no money to the schools. It does not support them. Its legislation, as applied, does no more than provide a general program to help parents get their children, regardless of their religion, safely and expeditiously to and from accredited schools."

This principle of equality of treatment for believers flows of necessity from the constitutional guarantee of religious liberty. If it were otherwise, a citizen would become, by reason of his religious belief, a second-class citizen. The First Amendment guarantees that religious belief shall not be cause for civil disabilities and for degradation to the level of second-class citizenship. Thomas Jefferson, the great exponent of civil liberties, emphasized this principle when he declared that "our civil rights have no dependence on our religious opinions."

The two principles incorporated in the voucher plan are identical with those incorporated in the old-age assistance program. First, in both the voucher plan and the old-age assistance program, government subsidizes the demand; it does not subsidize the supply. Second, in both, the individual who is subsidized is given complete freedom of choice to purchase particular needs in the open market place.

Government subsidizes the *demand* when it gives to individual citizens a money subsidy to purchase the commodity or commodities which the government, through its taxing power, is making available to a class of citizens. The subsidized individual citizen is given complete freedom of choice in purchasing the particular commodity or commodities in the open market.

Government subsidizes the *supply* when it subsidizes particular stores, or itself operates government stores, to supply a particular commodity or commodities to a particular class of individuals. The individuals for whom these benefits are intended have no freedom of choice. They have no alternative; they must accept the commodities provided by the government or they go without.

Not so many years ago the aged in need of government assistance were forced to go to state institutions for the needs of life. There they were compelled to accept the kind of meals, the kind of service, the kind of clothing the institutions provided. Freedom of choice in these matters was, for all practical purposes, nonexistent.

Today, however, in keeping with our respect for the dignity of the individual person, we have emancipated the needy aged from such government control over their physical needs. We have not done this by setting up government stores to distribute to the needy aged certain government selected brands of food and certain government selected fashions of clothing. This method, though it would relieve the aged of institutionalized living, would, nevertheless, still maintain complete government control over what the aged shall eat and what they shall wear. They would have no freedom of choice; their diet and apparel would be determined by government officials. There is unquestionably a servitude involved in the acceptance of such services and goods from the hands of government. It is incompatible with the dignity of the human person.

We have accomplished the emancipation of the needy aged by direct help to the individual person. We subsidize the demand. And the subsidized citizen is free to exercise his prerogative of choice in the purchase of his needs in the open market place.

The subsidized aged person may choose to purchase personally all of his needs and to live alone or with his family. Or he may choose to spend his subsidy to pay for subsistence with relatives or friends. Or, again, he may choose to spend the subsidy to pay for subsistence at some home for the aged operated by a particular religious group.

Under the old-age assistance program, thousands of our needy aged men and women have chosen to purchase their subsistent needs at denominational institutions. This purchase is made with money supplied by the Federal and state governments. In making this purchase in such institutions, they are exercising the freedom of choice guaranteed by the Social Security Act.

It is sometimes objected that the voucher method of subsidizing the education of children would involve government control of the schools the children choose to attend. This objection is based on the supposition that government control invariably follows the government dollar.

The objection can probably be best answered by an analysis of government activities in other programs in which it subsidizes the individual citizen.

When individual needy aged men and women purchase their needs at denominational institutions, does the government subsidize such institutions? If so, are the institutions subject to government control? These questions can, perhaps, most readily be answered by posing another question. When millions of individual needy aged men and women, using government subsidies, buy the needs of life at thousands of different private stores and shops throughout the nation, does the government subsidize these business enterprises? If so, are Macy's, Gimbels, Borden, the A&P, and Swift subject to government control?

The individual needy aged may take his government subsidy and shop with complete freedom at any store of his choice. The subsidy is not conditioned on the surrender of the freedom to purchase the physical needs of life wherever he prefers. Furthermore, the aged person may purchase whatever he desires. If for reasons of religious belief he does not wish to eat pork, it is not forced upon him by an intolerant government operating a government meat shop. The individual may purchase kosher meat, or he may purchase fish, or he may choose to dine exclusively on a vegetable diet; this is a personal matter and the government will not attempt to control his diet.

In 1961 the Federal Government and the several states subsidized the needy aged to the extent of $1,889,957,000. In that year 2,267,670 men and women received an average of $68.78 a month under the old-age program. This monthly subsidy is given to the individual person; it is not given to the store or market or denominational institution at which the individual needy aged purchases the commodities necessary for life.

The method adopted for providing for the needs of the aged men and women or our nation has a care for the dignity of their person and the independence of their individuality. They are not forcibly coerced to eat from a government table as a condition for sharing in government benefits.

The Federal Government subsidized the demand in another program adopted during the depression years of the 1930's. The government undertook to sub-sidize persons on relief to enable them to buy surplus foods. Relief clients could buy orange-colored stamps that could be used at a grocery store for the pur-chase of any kind of food. When he made the purchase of orange-colored stamps, he was *given* half as many blue-colored stamps which could be used for the purchase of goods in surplus. For every dollar that the citizen spent on food, the government gave him a half-dollar for the purchase of surplus food at the grocery of his choice.

When the government paid the grocer cash for both the orange and blue stamps that he had collected, did it subsidize the store? Here as in other welfare legislation the subsidy was made directly to the individual citizen exercising complete freedom of choice. The government did not subsidize the hundreds of thousands of private grocery stores across the nation. It subsidized the de-mand; it did not subsidize the supply.

If it should ever be established in law that in public welfare legislation govern-ment control must follow the public dollar, then we shall have gone a long way in setting up a totalitarian government. The government would then exercise control over a large portion of our private and corporate retail businesses. The Federal and state governments would not only exercise control over all the stores and shops at which approximately 2.3 million needy aged spend the Fed-eral-state dollar. But, using 1961 data, they would also control all the stores and shops at which the families or guardians of 2,764,500 dependent children spend a total of $1,235,456,000, at which 103,425 needy blind persons spend $93,236,000, and at which 395,530 permanently and totally disabled persons spend $317,-232,000 Federal-state dollars.

Does government have the right to control the private stores and shops at which the needy aged, the parents or guardians of dependent children, and the needy blind purchase with government subsidies, food, clothing, shelter, and other essential needs of life? True, the question sounds fantastic. Yet this is the logic of those who object to the voucher or tax credit plan on the grounds that a government subsidy for the individual child or student is a subsidy of the school attended and that such a subsidy would involve government control of independent schools.

Government control over the processes of education is far more objectionable than government control of businesses which supply the physical needs of life. If forced to choose between two so great evils as, on the one hand, government control of the kind and quality of food one must eat, and, on the other, of the kind and quality of thoughts one must think, surely no American who under-stands the importance of freedom of thought would hesitate in making his choice. Freedom can survive, to a considerable degree, even if government tells the citizen what brand of food he must eat and what fashion of clothes he must wear. But freedom cannot long survive when government tells him what thoughts he must think.

The philosophy that government control invariably follows the public dollar would destroy academic freedom. All universities receiving government grants for scientific and medical research would, all the more, fall under government control. All colleges and universities admitting veterans and war orphans would likewise fall under government control. And all colleges and universities admitting Federal fellowship and scholarship winners, if there are to be such, would also fall under government control.

The American people rejected this statist philosophy when they adopted legislation establishing both our social security programs and our educational and research programs.

The doctrine that government control invariable follows the public dollar is not a valid objection to the voucher plan. This doctrine has been rejected in all our social security programs, in all our educational programs for veterans, and, more recently, in our educational program for war orphans. And since freedom of the mind must be preserved, it must be rejected in future legislation in the field of education.

The reason for the rejection of this doctrine is apparent. These programs do not subsidize private business, they do not subsidize independent educational institutions; they subsidize the individual needy aged, the individual veteran, the individual war orphan. In a word, they do not subsidize the supply; they subsidize the demand. For this reason, also, as the President's Committee on Education Beyond the High School pointed out, the tax credit plan (and the same holds for the voucher plan) could be adopted "without raising the legal issue of 'church-state' relations."

Consequently, the voucher and tax credit plans, like these programs, do not raise constitutional questions. Any contention to the contrary is inconsistent with both law and practice.

Poindexter v. Louisiana Financial Assistance Commission

Throughout the 1960's, most of the pressure for unregulated vouchers came at the state level from parochial school groups in the North and segregationist forces in the South. The former were generally unsuccessful in obtaining legislative approval, whereas the latter succeeded in Virginia, Mississippi, Alabama, and Louisiana. None of these programs has survived judicial review. In these sections from the case on the Louisiana voucher (here called a tuition grant), a three-judge federal district court sets out the constitutional case against this kind of state program. This ruling was affirmed in a *per curiam* decision of the United States Supreme Court in 1968.

Other important voucher cases are: (1) Griffin v. State Board of Education, 377 U.S. 218 (1964); (2) Almond v. Day, 197 Va. 419 (1955); and (3) Swart v. Burlington, 122 Vt. 177 (1961).

275 F. Supp. 833 (1967)
U.S. District Court E.D. Louisiana, August 26, 1967

WISDOM, Circuit Judge:

This class action by Negro schoolchildren and their parents against the Louisiana Financial Assistance Commission and others attacks the constitutionality of Act 147 of 1962. Under that law the Commission administers a program of tuition grants to pupils attending private schools in Louisiana. The United States intervened as a party plaintiff; directors of four private schools for Negro retarded children intervened as parties defendant. . . .

The free lunches and textbooks Louisiana provides for all its school children are the fruits of racially neutral benevolence. Tuition grants are not the products of such a policy. They are the fruits of the State's traditional racially biased policy of providing segregated schools for white pupils. Here that policy has pushed the State to the extreme of using public funds to aid private discrimination endangering the public school system and equal educational opportunities for Negroes in Louisiana.

As certainly as "12" is the next number of a series starting 2, 4, 6, 8, 10, Act 147 fitted into the long series of statutes the Louisiana legislature enacted for over a hundred years to maintain segregated schools for white children. After the Supreme Court's 1954 decision in the School Segregation Cases, the legislature rapidly expanded the series. As fast as the courts knocked out one school law, the legislature enacted another. Each of these laws, whether its objective was obvious or nonobvious, was designed to provide a state-supported sanctuary for white children in flight from desegregated public schools.

Act 147 of 1962 is unconstitutional. The purpose and natural or reasonable effect of this law are to continue segregated education in Louisiana by providing state funds for the establishment and support of segregated, privately operated schools for white children. The United States Constitution does not permit the State to perform acts indirectly through private persons which it is forbidden to do directly. The evidence before the Court shows that the tuition grants have supplied a heavy predominance of funds needed to establish and maintain post-1954 and especially post-1962 private segregated schools. The

Commission's recent decision to reduce its aid to less than 50 per cent of the funds required for operating a school fails to take the curse off the Act. Any affirmative and purposeful state aid promoting private discrimination violates the equal protection clause. There is no such thing as the State's legitimately being just a little bit discriminatory.

The Statute   Act 147 of 1962 (LSA-R.S. 17:2951 –17:2953) authorizes state tuition grants for children attending "private non-sectarian elementary or secondary schools" in Louisiana. The statute creates the Louisiana Financial Assistance Commission to administer the program. The Commission is composed of three members appointed by the governor. Payments are "by check to the parent or guardian of, or the person standing in loco parentis to, the applicant." The statute is tied in with the public school system in the sense that to receive a grant, the applicants must be "eligible . . . for admission to elementary or secondary schools within the public school system of the state." Applicants must furnish "satisfactory evidence of admissibility to a private non-sectarian . . . school . . . legally constituted and operated under constitution and laws of the state." As thus far administered, each grant amounts to two dollars a day based on an assumed school term of 180 days, or $360, but limited to an amount not to exceed the tuition obligation actually incurred by the applicant. . . .

October 29, 1966, the Commission adopted a resolution stating, in part:

[T]he Commission has concluded that, except with respect to applicants on behalf of children attending private schools for retarded children, it will not pay tuition grants to applicants whose children attend any private school *predominantly* maintained through such tuition grants. In order to avoid unnecessary disruption of the present classes with consequent injury to the students, this policy shall be effective for school sessions commencing after June 1967.

The resolution was adopted to meet the holding in Griffin v. State Board of Education, E.D.Va.1965, 239 F.Supp. 560 (unappealed) and the definition of "public school" in the Civil Rights Act of 1964. *Griffin* held that state tuition grants are an unconstitutional application of a grant-in-aid law and discriminatory state action *only* when they "predominantly maintain" a segregated school. For purposes of Title IV (Public Education), the Civil Rights Act of 1964, § 401(c), defines "public school" as an institution "operated wholly or predominantly from or through the use of government funds or property." The Commission construes the resolution as authorizing payments to applicants attending a school supported by tuition grants which amount to any sum less than fifty per cent of the school's annual operating costs.

Purpose and Motive   We are not unmindful of the distinction courts draw between "purpose" and "motive." We accept the first Justice Harlan's statement, quoted by the defendants: "In a legal sense the object or purpose of legislation is to be determined by its natural and reasonable effect, whatever may have been the motive of the legislature."

There is no doubt that here the bottom problem, the situation at which Act 147 is aimed, is the desegregation of the public schools. The same problem had confronted other sessions of the legislature. Since 1958 the Louisiana legislative solution has been to offer the alternative of so-called "private" schools supported by state tuition grants. Public expressions by the legislators on the subject may or may not reveal the motives that actuated their vote. The Court is not interested in their motives. The Court is interested in their public expressions indicative of the legislative purpose, as the legislators understood the purpose of the legislation. . . .

In 1954, a few months after the Supreme Court decided the first *Brown* case desegregating public schools, Louisiana amended Article XII, Section 1 of the Constitution of 1921. This amendment expressed the state policy on segregated schools:

> All public elementary and secondary schools in the State of Louisiana shall be operated separately for white and colored children. This provision is made in the exercise of the state police power to promote and protect public health, morals, better education and the peace and good order in the State, and not because of race. The Legislature shall enact laws to enforce the state police power in this regard.

The Legislature promptly enacted Acts No. 555 and 556 of 1954. Act 555 carried out the constitutional requirement of separate schools and provided penalties for failing to observe it. Act 556 provided for the assignment to a school of each pupil each year by the superintendent of schools of the district in which the pupil lived. In February 1956 this Court held that both the amendment to Article XII Section 1 and the two statutes were invalid, and enjoined the Orleans Parish School Board from requiring and permitting segregation in the parish public schools. . . .

The Louisiana Legislature immediately enacted a new package of laws. Act 319 of 1956 purported to "freeze" the existing racial status of the public schools in Orleans Parish and to reserve to the legislature the power of racial reclassification of the schools. The Court declared this "legal artifice" unconstitutional on its face. . . .

In 1958 the legislature enacted another bundle of school laws.

Professor Charles A. Reynard of Louisiana State University has described these as follows:

> Adhering to its steadfast course of circumventing the Supreme Court's decisions forbidding the enforced segregation of the races in public education, the Legislature took steps to provide for the closing of public schools threatened with desegregation and authorized a system of publicly financed private education in lieu thereof. A pupil assignment law, applicable to the public schools, was also adopted. These measures were designed to fill the void created by the decisions of the federal courts invalidating acts adopted at the 1956 session, . . . which, in turn had been adopted to replace legislation passed in 1954, declared unconstitutional by the courts.

Act 257 provided in detail for the establishment of educational cooperatives. Act 258 established the first Louisiana system of grants-in-aid for "children attending non-sectarian non-public schools." Its purpose was obvious: The aid was conditioned on there being "no racially separate public school" in the parish. The grant system was to be administered jointly by the State Board of Education and the parish or city school boards.

By 1959 it was apparent to all that the Orleans Parish School Board could not take independent action to carry out the Court's order of February 15, 1956, requiring it to desegregate public schools in New Orleans. . . . When the Board failed to file a plan, the Court, on May 16, 1960, entered an order setting forth a plan of desegregation for the Orleans Parish School Board to follow. The plan called for the desegregation of the first grade in September 1960.

The Louisiana Legislature promptly built additional barricades. Act 333 of 1960 prohibited the furnishing of free books, school supplies, school funds or assistance to integrated schools. Act 495 authorized the Governor to close integrated schools. Act 496 purported to "freeze" the racial classification of public schools and reserve to the Legislature the power to change this classification. Act 542 authorized the Governor to close the public schools in case of riots and disorder.

The tempo of resistance increased. July 29, 1960, the Attorney General of Louisiana obtained an injunction in the state courts restraining the Orleans Parish School Board from desegregating its schools. August 17, 1960, the Governor of Louisiana, acting under Act 495 of 1960, took over control of the Orleans public schools. August 27, 1960, a three-judge district court struck down these actions. . . .

At this point, the Orleans School Board conferred with the district court. In public session the Board adopted a grade-a-year plan, postponed to November 14, 1960, and announced its intention to comply with the Court's orders.

The Board's compliance brought on five extraordinary sessions of the legislature within four months. Among other actions, the Legislature seized the funds of the Orleans Parish School Board; forbade banks to lend money to this Board; removed as fiscal agent for the state the Bank which honored payroll checks issued by the Orleans Board; ordered a school holiday on November 14, 1960; discharged four of the five Orleans Board members; later repealed the Act creating the Board, then twice created a new School Board for Orleans Parish; and still later discharged the Superintendent, dismissed the Board's attorney, and attempted to require that the State Attorney General be counsel for the Board. The courts declared these and other related acts unconstitutional. . . .

Act 3 of the Second Extraordinary Session of 1960 was the Legislature's second version of grants-in-aid. This law differs from Act 258 of 1958, which it repealed, in two respects. First, the legislature did away with the provision that availability of tuition grants was dependent on the integration of the public schools in the parish. Second, it restricted grants to non-profit schools. The administration of the grant system continued to be the joint responsibility of the State Board of Education and the parish or city school boards. On the day the Senate passed Act 3, State Senator E. W. Gravolet described the bill as designed to "dove-tail" with Act 257 of 1958, which authorized educational cooperatives, and commented that the grant-in-aid principle had been used successfully for a private school system in Prince Edward County, Virginia. At a meeting of the White Citizen's Council in New Orleans on December 15, 1960, the Secretary of State of Louisiana, Wade O. Martin, predicted that Louisiana would go from public to private schools so that every child would have a check or money to go to the school of his choice; the white schools would accept white students, and the "black schools" would accept Negro students. In the Louisiana House of Representatives. December 21, 1960, Representative Triche of Assumption Parish argued that the grant-in-aid system was the most effective weapon against the integration of public schools and that the tax was needed to continue the fight for a segregated school system in Louisiana.

In 1961 the Court of Appeals for the Fifth Circuit affirmed orders requiring the desegregation of public schools in East Baton Rouge and St. Helena Parishes. On the same day the Governor of Louisiana called the Second Extraordinary Session of the Legislature for 1961. He certified as emergency legislation what became Act 2 of that session. Act 2 masqueraded as a local option law. It gave each parish or municipal school board the "option" to close its schools if a majority of the qualified voters in the parish or municipality voted in favor of such action. The school board was then authorized to dispose of its property for such consideration as it deemed appropriate. Act 257 of 1958 had created educational cooperatives which could acquire the property and then operate schools with the state money furnished by the grant-in-aid program provided for in Act 3 of the Second Extraordinary Session of 1960. In Hall v. St. Helena the Court characterized the option for a poor parish such as St. Helena as an option to attend segregated schools—or no schools. . . .

Act 9 of the 1961 Second Extraordinary Session of 1961 transferred $2,500,-000 from the Public Welfare Fund to the Education Expense Grant Fund for grant-in-aid use. Act 10 of the same session transferred $200,000 monthly from the sales tax collections to the same fund for the same purpose.

In Hall v. St. Helena Parish School Board, . . . holding the grants-in-aid unconstitutional, the Court stated:

> Under Act 3 . . . the parish school boards would continue to supervise the "private" schools, under the State Board of Education, by administering the grant-in-aid program of tuition grants payable from state and local funds. . . .
>
> This analysis of Act 2 and related legislation makes it clear that when the Legislature integrated Act 2 with its companion measures, especially the "private" school acts, as part of a single carefully constructed design, constitutionally the design was self-defeating. Of necessity, the scheme requires such extensive state control, financial aid, and active participation that in operating the program the state would still be providing public education. [The state would not be doing business at the old stand, but the state would participate as the senior and not silent partner in the same sort of business.] The continuance of segregation at the state's public-private schools, therefore, is a violation of the equal protection clause.

This brings us to the 1961 session. First, the legislature repealed outright the state's compulsory school attendance law, Act 128. (Two years before, in Act 28 of 1956, the law was made inapplicable in a parish where the public school system had been ordered to integrate.) Act 342 of 1962 appropriated funds for the schools of St. Bernard Parish to compensate for expenses incurred in providing facilities for pupils who were not residents of St. Bernard; most of these were white students who had left the desegregated schools in neighboring Orleans Parish. Act 67 of 1962 purported to restrict the right to sue parish school boards, except by authorization of the Legislature.

This was the background and setting when the Louisiana Legislature enacted the statute under attack in this case. The Act transfers administration of tuition grants from the Board of Education to the Louisiana Financial Assistance Commission, provides that tuition grants be made directly to the parent rather than to the parent and school jointly and, to attract entrepreneurs, waives the requirement that schools attended by students receiving tuition grants be non-profit organizations. In all other significant respects Act 147 is substantially identical with the 1960 tuition grants statute.

In 1962 the legislative sponsors of Act 147 and some of the persons directly responsible for the operation of the grant-in-aid program were not reluctant to announce the purpose of the legislation.

State Senator E. W. Gravolet, Jr., was Senate Floor leader for the passage of the Act, vice-chairman of the Joint Legislature Committee on Segregation, and Chairman of the Financial Assistance Commission from its inception. He stated:

> It was primarily because of that federal court decision, [Hall v. St. Helena Parish School Board] combined with the one in Virginia that the Louisiana Legislature took away the administration of the tuition grants from the State Board of Education and the local school boards and created a new commission to disburse the tuition grants directly to the child, following the constitutional theory that grants directly to the child by the states were legal.

> The federal court went out of its way in the *St. Helena* case to point out that grant-in-aid could be attacked as being state action under the 14th amendment of the United States Constitution if they were administered by the local school board, because the various private schools would be classified by federal courts as private-public schools.

Immediately after Act 147 had been passed, Senator Gravolet described the establishment of the defendant Commission as a means to give citizens a choice whether they want to send their children to desegregated schools. He said, further, that if any large number of Negroes enroll at either public or parochial schools "we may have a lot of makeshift cooperative schools." His reference was to so-called educational cooperatives, private nonsectarian schools, the establishment of which were made possible by LSA-R.S. 17:2801, enacted on the same day as Act 258 of 1958, the first tuition grant statute. Shortly thereafter, Gravolet, as newly appointed Chairman of the Commission, said that he understood the Commission would establish a brand new state department with a permanent staff to channel state funds to applicants seeking to avoid integrated schools by attending private nonsectarian schools.

In a letter which Senator Gravolet signed as Chairman of the Commission, distributed in January of 1964, during the second gubernatorial primary election, he stated, in full:

> I enclose a New Orleans clipping showing Morrison's statement that he is unalterably opposed to state grant-in-aid to help your children go to a private segregated school of your choice, instead of having to go to a racially integrated school.

Your only hope to continue to get school checks to help your children go to private schools is by electing John McKeithen governor on Saturday, January 11.

E. W. Gravolet, Jr.
Chairman
Louisiana Financial
Assistance Commission

The Vice-Chairman of the Commission, Representative Lantz Womack, stated to a Citizens Council meeting in New Orleans on December 4, 1963, that the grant-in-aid program was started in 1958 "but very little use was made of it until the integration move began in New Orleans." ...

The present Louisiana tuition statute, like its counterpart in Alabama, was "designed to fill the vacuum left by this Court's injunction against the [earlier] tuition statute." Waiting in the wings to play the role Act 147 is forbidden to play is Act 99 of 1967. The 1967 substitute provides "financial aid scholarships to needy children enrolled in private non-sectarian elementary and secondary schools located in this state *whose parents choose not to enroll said children in the public education facilities of this state,*" because they are "mindful of the increase in juvenile delinquency, school dropouts and juvenile crime rates ... mindful that the parent, not the State of Louisiana, shall be the determining force which shall decide on the type of education ultimately received by the child ... [but] lack the finances which would enable them to enroll their children in private schools."

Thus, for a hundred years, the Louisiana legislature has not deviated from its objective of maintaining segregated schools for white children. Ten years after *Brown*, declared policy became undeclared policy. Open legislative defiance of desegregation orders shifted to subtle forms of circumvention—although some prominent sponsors of grant-in-aid legislation have been less than subtle in their public expression. But the changes in means reflect no change in legislative ends.

Effect of Act 147   The problem of fairly ascertaining the effect of a statute becomes complicated when the degree of a state's involvement in private discrimination is nonobvious. In Burton v. Wilmington Parking Authority, 1961, 365 U.S. 715, the Supreme Court observed, "Only by sifting facts and weighing circumstances can the nonobvious involvement of the State in private conduct be attributed its true significance."

In our earlier opinion in this case we held that "any amount of state support to help found segregated schools or to help maintain such schools is sufficient to give standing to Negro school children to file the kind of complaint filed in this case." We concluded, however, largely because of *Burton:*

> This case should be decided after a full trial of the facts. The extent to which the tuition grants contributed to the founding of the quasi-public schools, in dollars and as a stimulus, the extent to which the grants now contribute to the support of the quasi-public schools, the extent of state involvement and control, and other factors relevant to state action can be determined only by a trial on the merits.

The inevitable effect of the tuition grants was the establishment and maintenance of a state-supported system of segregated schools for white children, making the state a party to organized private discrimination.

There are 67 school districts in Louisiana, 15 of which were not, at the opening of the 1966-67 school year, under court order to desegregate. There are 79 private, nonsectarian schools in nine school districts. In seven of these school districts private schools were formed after enactment of Act 147: East Feliciana, East Baton Rouge, Jefferson, Orleans, St. Tammany, Bogalusa (Washington), Plaquemines. In these districts public schools are desegregated by court order. Of the 79 schools, 62 are for normal children: 60 for white pupils, two for Negro pupils. Each of these schools is segregated.

Before 1954 there were 16 private schools in the state, all but one located within the New Orleans Metropolitan area. After 1954 but before enactment of the 1960 tuition grant statute, nine additional schools were started. Between enactment of the 1960 law and enactment of Act 147 in July 1962, eight more private schools came into being. Between the enactment of Act 147 and the time of the trial of this case, 36 additional schools for white children began operation. Thus 44 of the 60 private schools for white children were formed after the first desegregation of public schools in 1960.

The amounts the newly organized schools charge for tuition show that these schools could not have come into existence and could not have continued to exist without the state's grants-in-aid. . . .

The directors and principals of thirty-two private schools were deposed and questioned about their admissions policy. All but six were equivocal in their statements. The statements of many of these principals that they maintained no policy as to the admission of Negroes must come as a surprise and shock to the parents who have children attending these schools. We find such statements incredible.

Two others, while stating that they would accept a Negro applicant who met their requirements, said that their schools had very stringent social and moral qualifications. Indeed, the Garden District Academy requires as a prerequisite to admission, the recommendations of two patrons of the school. All of the patrons are white. A similar requirement, maintained by the University of Mississippi was held to constitute racial discrimination in Meredith v. Fair.

Of the six who gave definite answers, five stated that their schools were open only to Caucasians. The remaining deponent stated that she would accept any Negro child who met the standards required of white students.

More credible is the testimony of Charles LaCoste, former director of the Carrollton Elementary School. He testified that the basic purpose for the organization of the school was to avoid public school desegregation and that the existence of tuition grants allowed that purpose to be accomplished. Further, he testified that after public schools were desegregated in New Orleans, his group met with Armond J. Duvio, one of the chief organizers of private schools in New Orleans. In these meetings, the group discussed tuition grants and public school desegregation in relation to the formation of the private schools. . . .

In effect the state has established a second system of schools, competitive with the public school system. The public schools no doubt will survive such competition, but only after sustaining severe damage detrimental to the system and to students attending public schools. For example, of the 345 teachers in private schools organized since 1962, 139 teachers or 35% came from the public schools.

There are 5,187 white children in pre-1954 private schools. 3,483 receive grants although many attend expensive, fashionable, endowed schools, such as the Louise McGehee School for Girls, Newman School, and Metairie Park Country Day School.

There are 4,029 students attending private schools formed between 1954 and enactment of Act 147; 3,336 receive grants. Attending schools formed after enactment of Act 147 are 7,376 white children, of whom 6,874 receive grants; 386 Negro children, of whom 366 receive grants. In the seven districts where private schools were formed after 1962, there are 244,158 students enrolled in the public schools; 7,762 students enrolled in the private schools, of whom 7,240 receive grants. *It is a fair inference that these substantial numbers of white students at private schools represent only a small fraction of the number that will enroll in such schools, should the courts bless the state tuition grant program.*

In brief, the evidence produced in court of the actual effect of Act 147 substantiates the view of the purpose and the natural or reasonable effect of the law to be inferred from an understanding of Act 147 in its historical context and legislative setting. The tuition grants authorized under the Act provided the funds indispensable to establishing newly organized private segregated schools for white children. The tuition grants continue to furnish almost all of the funds needed for maintaining these post-Brown schools. What Hall v.

St. Helena forbade the State to do directly, it has attempted to accomplish indirectly. The tuition grants damage Negroes by draining students, teachers, and funds from the desegregated public school system into a competitive, segregated "quasi-public" school system. The stamp of State approval of "white" schools perpetuates the open humiliation of the Negro implicit in segregated education.

The Defendants' Authorities; Lee v. Macon County; The Griffin Test   The defendants insist that Act 147 stands alone, and that it is constitutional on its face and as applied.

Defendants' counsel resort to history, going back to colonial times, to trace the record of public assistance to private schools. But as we noted in our discussion of the statutory purpose (Section II of this opinion), the overriding constitutional principle here is that "acts generally lawful may become unlawful when done to accomplish an unlawful end." The unlawful end and necessary effect of the Louisiana tuition grants were to establish and maintain a system of segregated schools for white children, in violation of the equal protection clause.

In support of their contention, counsel cite Meyer v. Nebraska, 1923, Pierce v. Society of the Sisters, 1925, Cochran v. Louisiana State Board of Education, 1930, and Everson v. Board of Education, 1947. *Meyer*, a due process case, held that a state law prohibiting the teaching of "any subject to any person in any language other than the English language" is "arbitrary or without reasonable relation to some purpose within the competency of the State." The Court observed, "Determination by the Legislature of what constitutes proper exercise of police power is not final or conclusive but is subject to supervision by the courts." In *Pierce* an Oregon statute in effect prohibited private elementary schools by requiring children between the ages of eight and sixteen to attend public schools. The Court held that the statute violated due process in unreasonably interfering with the liberty of parents by forcing their children to accept instruction from public teachers only. *Cochran* involved state-supplied schoolbooks, *Everson* state-supplied bus transportation to all pupils. In these two cases, the question was whether the expenditure of public funds for private purposes violated the due process clause. In each case the Court recognized that the taxing power of the state was exerted for a public purpose.

The shafts cut from these due process decisions miss their target. None of these cases involved the equal protection clause. The Supreme Court had very little difficulty in *Cochran* and in *Everson* in recognizing a public purpose in legislation facilitating the opportunity of children to get a secular education. But in *Cochran* the Court pointed out, "The schools, however, are not the beneficiaries of these appropriations...." And in *Everson* the Court pointed out, "The fact that a state law, passed to satisfy a public need, coincides with the personal desires of the individuals most directly affected is certainly an inadequate reason for us to say that a legislature has erroneously appraised a public need." On the facts before us, the private schools established in Louisiana are direct beneficiaries of the grants-in-aid; the children or the parents are conduits to the schools.

The 1958 program invalidated in Hall v. St. Helena Parish School Board allowed parish school boards to close public schools under desegregation orders and to lease the buildings to private persons and cooperatives. The present program funnels public funds into the hands of private persons who are thereby enabled to provide different school buildings but count on having the same students and teachers. The 1962 plan has the same purpose and many of the effects of the 1958 plan.

A parallel development took place in Alabama, which has also had three successive tuition grants programs. In 1956 Alabama authorized each local board of education to close public schools when it found that continued operation of the schools would "be accompanied by such tensions, friction, or potential disorder or ill will within the school as substantially to impair effective standards or objectives of education of its pupils." This statute, like the 1958 Louisiana law, authorized tuition grants for students attending private nondenominational schools in districts where no public school was available. In 1964 a three-judge court in Lee v. Macon County Board of Education held that the law was unconstitutional. In 1965, Alabama, like Louisiana, adopted a more refined substitute for the earlier version. This new statute was cast in terms of making eligibility turn on the parent's judgment that the child's attendance at public school would be detrimental to the child's "physical and emotional health." In 1967, in the most recent decision in Lee v. Macon County, the same three-judge court held: The tuition grant statute was "designed to aid and assist private discrimination of the kind that would be condemned if attempted by the state. As such the statute is unconstitutional." . . .

The Virginia system of tuition grants was invalidated in Griffin v. State Board of Education. The Virginia tuition statute authorized grants of $125 a year for elementary pupils and $150 a year for high school students. This money came from the State Treasury. In addition, each local school board could pay each child an amount equal to the amount the State provided. A three-judge court stated, and we agree:

> With the plaintiffs, we think the State cannot ignore any plain misuse to which a grant has been or is intended to be put. Nor do we think weight is to be accorded the fact that the money is paid to the pupil or parent and not to the school, for the pupil or parent is a mere channel. . . . These premises of decision have especial significance here because the issue is the right of

the State or locality to make, and not the right of the pupils, parents or schools to take, the grants.

The court found, "incontestably, that the grants are the main support" of each of the segregated schools:

This contribution is of such relative magnitude that they plainly are State supported institutions. Thus the State is nurturing segregated schools. Hence, the defendants must be enjoined from providing money to be funnelled by the parents into these schools so long as segregation is practiced in them.

We have made a similar finding and reached a similar result in this case.

In *Griffin*, however, the court held that the Virginia tuition grant statute was not unconstitutional on its face and that, as administered, the tuition grants are unconstitutional only because they "predominantly maintain" a segregated school. The court said:

Payment of a tuition grant for use in a private school is legal if it does not tend in a determinative degree to perpetuate segregation. The test is not the policy of the school, but the measure in which the grant or grants contribute to effect the exclusion on account of race. Every exclusive school is not a forbidden school. The part played by the grant in effectuating the exclusion, to repeat, is the pivotal point. It is decisive because the extent of such participation determines whether or not the exclusion is State action—the fundamental question here.... Our determination is simply that the preponderant support of a segregated school may not be rooted in State action.

Because of the "predominance" test adopted in *Griffin* and in the Civil Rights Act, the Louisiana Commission adopted its resolution limiting grants, after June 1967, to applicants attending schools not "predominantly maintained" by state tuition grants. The Commission argues strongly that, at least from now on, the resolution cures any unconstitutional effect or application of the law.

With deference, we disagree with the criterion the Court applied in *Griffin*. The payment of public funds in any amount through a state commission under authority of a state law is undeniably state action. The question is whether such action in aid of private discrimination violates the equal protection clause.

When state funds predominantly support a private segregated school and when such a school, by congressional act, may be described as a "public school" for certain purposes of the Civil Rights Act of 1964, the state involvement is a double *fortiori* case of unconstitutional state action. But decisions on the constitutionality of state involvement in private discrimination do not turn on whether the state aid adds up to 51 per cent or adds up only to 49 per cent of the support of the segregated institution. The criterion is whether the state is so *significantly* involved in the private discrimination as to render the state action and the private action violative of the equal protection clause. (Here the plaintiffs ask only that the state be enjoined from paying the tuition grants; not that the schools be desegregated.)

The courts have wisely not attempted to devise a formula that would include "significant involvement" in all types of private discrimination. In the Little Rock case the Supreme Court said, "State support of segregated schools *through any arrangement*, management, funds, or property cannot be squared with the Fourteenth Amendment's command that no State shall deny to any person within its jurisdiction the equal protection of the laws." Cooper v. Aaron, 1958. In Lee v. Macon County the court said that the State, through tuition grants, may not "induce, encourage or promote private persons to accomplish what it is constitutionally forbidden to accomplish." The court in that case, properly we think, focused on the State's approval or sponsorship of private segregated schools. The constitutional odium of official approval of race discrimination has no necessary relation to the extent of the State's financial support of a discriminatory institution. Any aid to segregated schools that is the product of the State's affirmative, purposeful policy of fostering segregated schools and has the effect of encouraging discrimination is significant state involvement in private discrimination. (We distinguish, therefore, state aid from tax benefits, free schoolbooks, and other products of the State's traditional policy of benevolence toward charitable and educational institutions.) ...

As the Supreme Court noted in Reitman v. Mulkey, the "Court has never attempted the 'impossible task' of formulating an infallible test for determining whether the State 'in any of its manifestations' has become significantly involved in private discriminations." The facts must be sifted and weighed on a case-to-case basis. The cases in this area of the law teach, however, that there is no constitutional basis for courts to adopt as a test the predominance of state financial support. The State's only involvement in *Burton* was as lessor. It was very slight in *Simkins*. In Anderson v. Martin and Reitman v. Mulkey, there was no state financial involvement.

In *Griffin* the Court warned that private schools receiving tuition grants might be ordered to desegregate. "[C]ontinued predominantly State or local government support of the private schools herein mentioned might expose some of the defendants to subsequent suit under the [Civil Rights] Act." In Lee v. Macon County, the Court issued a similar warning based on the State's "significant involvement." The court did not refer to the Civil Rights Act definition or to the Griffin test. The Court found that Alabama was attempting to "support a separate and private school system for white students." "Moreover, the Governor has officially encouraged private contributions to support the many private schools throughout the state *as alternatives to the public de-segregated school system."* The Court warned, "if the state persisted, and if its involvement with the private school system continues to be 'significant', then this 'private' system will have become a state factor within the meaning of the Fourteenth Amendment and will need to be brought under this Court's state-wide desegregation order." . . .

Griffin, one of the cases handed down with *Brown* in 1954, concerned the public schools in Prince Edward County, Virginia. In 1964 the Supreme Court held that the Virginia statute providing tuition grants, when coupled with closing of the public schools, denied Negroes an integrated education. "The same reasoning applies when the grants alone deny Negroes an integrated public education by assisting whites to flee to private schools. It is impossible to set a standard as to the number of whites who may leave before the schools become segregated, but state-encouraged departure of any whites tends to create segregation, and it would seem that any state support of segregation violates the equal protection clause." This conclusion is consistent with the principle expressed in Cooper v. Aaron that State support of segregated schools "through any arrangement, management, funds, or property cannot be squared with the [Fourteenth] Amendment." And it is consistent with the principle expressed in Lee v. Macon County that the State may not "induce, encourage or promote private persons to accomplish what it is constitutionally forbidden to accomplish."

We summarize.

The system of private segregated schools the State created and nourishes through Act 147 is in a nascent stage. Its tangible and intangible costs to the State *thus far* are but a drop in the bucket compared with its future costs—should the courts bless the nourishment the private schools receive from the State. The facts this case presents point in only one direction: Unless this system is destroyed, it will shatter to bits the public school system of Louisiana and kill the hope that now exists for equal educational opportunities for all our citizens, white and black.

We hold that the purpose and natural or reasonable effect of Act 147 of 1962 render it unconstitutional on its face. The law was designed to establish and maintain a system of segregated schools. We hold also that Act 147 of 1962 is unconstitutional in its actual effect. The State has predominantly supplied the financial means necessary to establish and maintain the post-1962 private schools and most of the post-1954 private schools in Louisiana. The State is so significantly involved in the discrimination practiced by the private schools in Louisiana that any financial aid from the State to these schools or newly organized schools in the form of tuition grants or similar benefits violates the equal protection clause of the Fourteenth Amendment. . . .

PART II

The Regulated Voucher

Education Vouchers: A Proposal for Diversity and Choice

Judith Areen is a fellow at the Center for the
Study of Public Policy (CSPP) in Cambridge
and an instructor at Boston University
School of Law. Christopher Jencks is
co-director of the Center and associate
professor of education at Harvard University.
In this essay, the authors set out the basic
contentions for a regulated voucher system
of the type that the Office of Economic
Opportunity is now supporting.

Judith Areen
Christopher Jencks

Ever since Adam Smith first proposed that the government finance education by giving parents money to hire teachers, the idea has enjoyed recurrent popularity. Smith's ideal of consumer sovereignty is built into a number of government programs for financing higher education, notably the G. I. Bill and the various state scholarship programs. Similarly a number of foreign countries have recognized the principle that parents who are dissatisfied with their local public school should be given money to establish alternatives.[1] In America, however, public financing for elementary and secondary education has been largely confined to publicly managed schools. Parents who preferred a private alternative have had to pay the full cost out of their own pockets. As a result, we have almost no evidence on which to judge the merit of Smith's basic principle namely, that if all parents are given the chance, they will look after their children's interests more effectively than will the state.

During the late 1960s, a series of developments in both public and nonpublic education led to a revival of interest in this approach to financing education. In December, 1969, the United States Office of Economic Opportunity made a grant to the Center for the Study of Public Policy to support a detailed study of "education vouchers." This article will summarize the major findings of that report and outline briefly the voucher plan proposed by the Center.[2]

The Case for Choice Conservatives, liberals, and radicals all have complained at one time or another that the political mechanisms which supposedly make public schools accountable to their clients work clumsily and ineffectively.[3] Parents who think their children are getting inferior

1 Estelle Fuchs, "The Free Schools of Denmark," *Saturday Review*, August 16, 1969.
2 For a complete description of the Center proposal, *see Education Vouchers: A Report on Financing Education by Payments to Parents*. Prepared by the Center for the Study of Public Policy, Cambridge, Massachusetts, December, 1970.
3 For other discussions of the need to encourage alternatives tc the present public schools, *see* Kenneth Clark, "Alternative Public School Systems," *Equal Educational Opportunity*. Cambridge: Harvard University Press, 1969; James S. Coleman, "Toward Open

schooling can, it is true, take their grievances to the local school board or state legislature. If legislators and school boards are unresponsive to the complaints of enough citizens, they may eventually be unseated. But mounting an effective campaign to change local public schools takes an enormous investment of time, energy, and money. Dissatisfied though they may be, few parents have the political skill or commitment to solve their problems this way. As a result, effective control over the character of the public schools is largely vested in legislators, school boards, and educators—not parents.[4]

If parents are to take genuine responsibility for their children's education, they cannot rely exclusively on political processes. They must also be able to take individual action on behalf of their own children. At present, only relatively affluent parents retain any effective control over the education of their children. Only they are free to move to areas with "good" public schools, where housing is usually expensive (and often unavailable to black families at any price). Only they can afford nonsectarian, private schooling. The average parent has no alternative to his local public school unless he happens to belong to one of the few denominations that maintain low-tuition schools.

Not only does today's public school have a captive clientele, but it in turn has become the captive of a political process designed to protect the interests of its clientele. Because attendance at a local public school is nearly compulsory, its activities have been subjected to extremely close political control. The state, the local board, and the school administration have established regulations to ensure that no school will do anything to offend anyone of political consequence. Virtually everything of consequence is either forbidden or compul-

---

Schools," *The Public Interest*, Fall, 1967; Anthony Downs, "Competition and Community Schools," written for a Brookings Institution Conference on the Community School held in Washington, D.C., December 12-13, 1968, Chicago, Illinois, revised version, January, 1969; Milton Friedman, "The Role of Government in Education," *Capitalism and Freedom*. Chicago: University of Chicago Press, 1962; Christopher Jencks, "Is the Public School Obsolete?" *The Public Interest*, Winter, 1966; Robert Krughoff, "Private Schools for the Public," *Education and Urban Society*, Vol. II, November, 1969; Henry M. Levin, "The Failure of the Public Schools and the Free Market," *The Urban Review*, June 6, 1968; Theodore Sizer and Phillip Whitten, "A Proposal for a Poor Children's Bill of Rights," *Psychology Today*, August, 1968; E. G. West. *Education and the State*. London: Institute of Economic Affairs, 1965.

4 School management has been increasingly concentrated in the hands of fewer educators and school boards. The number of school districts, for example, declined from 127,531 in 1930, to less than 20,440 in 1968. The number of public elementary schools dropped from 238,000 to less than 73,000 in the same period. The concentration is particularly striking in urban areas. The New York City School Board alone is responsible for the education of more students than are found in the majority of individual states. Los Angeles has as many students as the state of South Carolina; Chicago as many as Kansas; Detroit as many as Maine. Nearly half of all the students in public schools are under the control of less than 4 percent of the school boards. *See*, U.S. Department of Health, Education, and Welfare, Digest of Educational Statistics (1969).

sory. By trying to please everyone, however, the schools have often ended up pleasing no one.

A voucher system seeks to free schools from the restrictions which inevitably accompany their present monopolistic privileges. The idea of the system is relatively simple. A publicly accountable agency would issue a voucher to parents. The parents could take this voucher to any school which agreed to abide by the rules of a voucher system. Each school would turn its vouchers in for cash. Thus parents would no longer be forced to send their children to the school around the corner simply because it was around the corner.

Even if no new schools were established under a voucher system, the responsiveness of existing public schools would probably increase. We believe that one of the most important advantages of a voucher system is that it would encourage diversity and choice *within the public system.* Indeed, if the public system were to begin matching students and schools on the basis of interest, rather than residence, one of the major objectives of a voucher system would be met without even involving the private sector. Popular public schools would get more applicants, and they would also have incentives to accommodate them, since extra students would bring extra funds. Unpopular schools would have few students, and would either have to change their ways or close up and reopen under new management.

As this last possibility suggests, however, there are great advantages to involving the private sector in a voucher system if it is properly regulated. Only in this way is the overall system likely to make room for fundamentally new initiatives that come from the bottom instead of the top. And only if private initiative is possible will the public sector feel real pressure to make room for kinds of education that are politically awkward but have a substantial constituency. If the private sector is involved, for example, parents can get together to create schools reflecting their special perspectives or their children's special needs. This should mean that the public schools will be more willing to do the same thing—though they will never be willing or able to accommodate *all* parental preferences. Similarly if the private sector is involved, educators with new ideas—or old ideas that are now out of fashion in the public schools— would also be able to set up their own schools Entrepreneurs who thought they could teach children better and more inexpensively than the public schools would have an opportunity to do so. None of this ensures that every child would get the education he needs, but it would make such a result somewhat more likely than at present.

Beyond this, however, differences of opinion begin. Who would be eligible for vouchers? How would their value be determined? Would parents be allowed to supplement the vouchers from their own funds? What requirements would schools have to meet before cashing vouchers? What arrangements would be made for the children whom no school wanted to educate? Would church schools be eligible? Would schools promoting unorthodox political views be eligible? Once the advocates of vouchers begin to answer such questions, it becomes clear that the catch phrase around which they have united stands not for a single panacea, but for a multitude of controversial programs, many of which have little in common.

Revised Vocabulary   To understand the voucher plan recommended by the Center, it is useful to begin by reconsidering traditional notions about "public" and "private" education. Since the nineteenth century, we have classified schools as "public" if they were owned and operated by a governmental body. We go right on calling colleges "public," even when they charge tuition that many people cannot afford. We also call academically exclusive high schools "public," even if they have admissions requirements that only a handful of students can meet. We call neighborhood schools "public," despite the fact that nobody outside the neighborhood can attend them, and nobody can move into the neighborhood unless he has white skin and a down payment on a $30,000 home. And we call whole school systems "public," even though they refuse to give anyone information about what they are doing, how well they are doing it, and whether children are getting what their parents want. Conversely, we have always called schools "private" if they were owned and operated by private organizations. We have gone on calling these schools "private," even when, as sometimes happens, they are open to every applicant on a nondiscriminatory basis, charge no tuition, and make whatever information they have about themselves available to anyone who asks.

Definitions of this kind conceal as much as they reveal, for they classify schools entirely in terms of *who* runs them, not *how* they are run. If we want to describe what is really going on in education, there is much to be said for reversing this emphasis. We would then call a school "public" if it were open to everyone on a nondiscriminatory basis, if it charged no tuition, and if it provided full information about itself to anyone interested. Conversely, we would call any school "private" if it excluded applicants in a discriminatory way, charged tuition, or withheld information about itself. Admittedly, the question of who governs a school cannot be ignored entirely when categorizing the school, but it seems considerably less important than the question of how the school is governed.

Adopting this revised vocabulary, we propose a regulatory system with two underlying principles:

—No public money should be used to support "private" schools.
—Any group that operates a "public" school should be eligible for public subsidies.

The Proposal Specifically, the Center has proposed an education voucher system (for *elementary* education) which would work in the following manner:

1. An Educational Voucher Agency (EVA) would be established to administer the vouchers. Its governing board might be elected or appointed, but in either case it should be structured so as to represent minority as well as majority interests. The EVA might be an existing local board of education, or it might be an agency with a larger or smaller geographic jurisdiction. The EVA would receive all federal, state, and local education funds for which children in its area were eligible. It would pay this money to schools only in return for vouchers. (In addition, it would pay parents for children's transportation costs to the school of their choice.)

2. The EVA would issue a voucher to every family in its district with children of elementary school age. The value of the basic voucher would initially equal the per pupil expenditure of the public schools in the area. Schools which took children from families with below-average incomes would receive additional incentive payments. These "compensatory payments" might, for example, make the maximum payment for the poorest child worth double the basic voucher.

3. To become an "approved voucher school," eligible to cash vouchers, a school would have to:

   a. Accept each voucher as full payment for a child's education, charging no additional tuition.
   b. Accept any applicant so long as it had vacant places.
   c. If it had more applicants than places, fill at least half these places by picking applicants randomly and fill the other half in such a way as not to discriminate against ethnic minorities.
   d. Accept uniform standards established by the EVA regarding suspension and expulsion of students.
   e. Agree to make a wide variety of information about its facilities, teachers, program, and students available to the EVA and to the public.
   f. Maintain accounts of money received and disbursed in a form that would allow both parents and the EVA to determine where the money was going. Thus a school operated by the local board of education (a "public" school) would have to show how much of the money to which it was entitled on the basis of its vouchers was actually spent in that school. A school operated by a profit-making corporation would have to show how much of its income was going to the stockholders.
   g. Meet existing state requirements for *private* schools regarding curriculum, staffing, and the like.

Control over policy in an approved voucher school might be vested in an existing local school board, a PTA, or any private group. Hopefully, no government restrictions would be placed on curriculum, staffing, and the like, except those already established for all private schools in a state.

4. Just as at present, the local board of education (which might or might not be the EVA) would be responsible for ensuring that there were enough places in publicly managed schools to accommodate every elementary school age child who did not want to attend a privately managed school. If a shortage of places developed for some reason, the board of education would have to open new schools or create more places in existing schools. (Alternatively, it might find ways to encourage privately managed schools to expand, presumably by getting the EVA to raise the value of the voucher.)

5. Every spring each family would submit to the EVA the name of the school to which it wanted to send each of its elementary school age children next fall. Any children already enrolled in a voucher school would be guaranteed a place, as would any sibling of a child enrolled in a voucher school. So long as it had room, a voucher school would be required to admit all students who listed it as a first choice. If it did not have room for all applicants, a school could fill half its places in whatever way it wanted, choosing among those who listed it as a first choice. It could not, however, select these applicants in such a way as to discriminate against racial minorities. It would then have to fill its remaining places by a lottery among the remaining applicants. All schools with unfilled places would report these to the EVA. All families whose children had not been admitted to their first-choice school would then choose an alternative school which still had vacancies. Vacancies would then be filled in the same manner as in the first round. This procedure would continue until every child had been admitted to a school.

6. Having enrolled their children in a school, parents would give their vouchers to the school. The school would send the vouchers to the EVA and would receive a check in return.

Some Caveats   The voucher system outlined above is quite different from other systems now being advocated; it contains far more safeguards for the interests of disadvantaged children. A voucher system which does not include these or equally effective safeguards would be worse than no voucher system at all. Indeed, an unregulated voucher system could be the most serious setback for the education of disadvantaged children in the history of the United States. A properly regulated system, on the other hand, may have the potential to inaugurate a new era of innovation and reform in American schools.

One common objection to a voucher system of this kind is that many parents are too ignorant to make intelligent choices among schools. Giving parents a choice will, according to this argument, simply set in motion an educational equivalent of Gresham's Law, in which hucksterism and mediocre schooling drive out high quality institutions. This argument seems especially plausible to those who envisage the entry of large numbers of profit-oriented firms into the educational marketplace. The argument is not, however, supported by much evidence. Existing private schools are sometimes mere diploma mills, but on the average their claims about themselves seem no more misleading, and the quality of the services they offer no lower, than in the public schools. And while some private schools are run by hucksters interested only in profit, this is the exception rather than the rule. There is no obvious reason to suppose that vouchers would change all this.

A second common objection to vouchers is that they would "destroy the public schools." Again, this seems far-fetched. If you look at the educational choices made by wealthy parents who can already afford whatever schooling they want for their children, you find that most still prefer their local public schools if these are at all adequate. Furthermore, most of those who now leave the public system do so in order to attend high-cost, exclusive private schools. While some wealthy parents would doubtless continue to patronize such schools, they would receive no subsidy under the proposed system.

Nonetheless, if you are willing to call every school "public" that is ultimately responsible to a public board of education, then there is little doubt that a voucher system would result in some shrinkage of the "public" sector and some growth of the "private" sector. If, on the other hand, you confine the label "public" to schools which are equally open to everyone within commuting distance, you discover that the so-called public sector includes relatively few public schools. Instead, racially exclusive suburbs and economically exclusive neighborhoods serve to ration access to good "public" schools in precisely the same way that admissions committees and tuition charges ration access to good "private" schools. If you begin to look at the distinction between public and private schooling in these terms, emphasizing accessibility rather than control, you are likely to conclude that a voucher system, far from destroying the public sector, would greatly expand it, since it would force large numbers of schools, public and private, to open their doors to outsiders.

A third objection to vouchers is that they would be available to children attending Catholic schools. This is not, of course, a necessary feature of a voucher system. The courts, a state legislature, or a local EVA could easily restrict participation to nonsectarian schools. Indeed, some state constitutions clearly require that this be done. The federal Constitution may also require such a restriction, but neither the language of the First Amendment nor the legal precedent is clear on this issue. The First Amendment's prohibition against an "establishment of religion" can be construed as barring payments to church schools, but the "free exercise of religion" clause can also be construed as requiring the state to treat church schools in precisely the same way as other private schools. The Supreme Court has never ruled on a case of this type (e.g., G.I. Bill payments to Catholic colleges or Medicare payments to Catholic hospitals). Until it does, the issue ought to be resolved on policy grounds. And since the available evidence indicates that Catholic schools have served their children no worse than public schools,[5] and perhaps slightly better, there seems no compelling reason to deny them the same financial support given other schools.

(4)   The most worrisome objection to a voucher system is that its success would depend on the EVA's willingness to regulate the marketplace vigorously. If vouchers were used on a large scale, state and local regulatory efforts might be uneven or even nonexistent. The regulations designed to prevent racial and economic discrimination seem especially likely to get watered down at the state and local level, or else to remain unenforced. This argument applies, however, to *any* educational reform, and it also applies to the existing system. If you assume any given EVA will be controlled by overt or covert segregationists, you must also assume that this will be true of the local board of education. A board of education that wants to keep racist parents happy hardly needs vouchers to do so. It only needs to maintain the neighborhood school system. White parents who want their children to attend white schools will then find it quite simple to move to a white neighborhood where their children will be suitably segregated. Except perhaps in the South, neither the federal government, the state government, nor the judiciary is likely to prevent this traditional practice.

If, on the other hand, you assume a board which is anxious to eliminate segregation, either for legal, financial, or political reasons, you must also assume that the EVA would be subject to the same pressures. And if an EVA is anxious to eliminate segregation, it will have no difficulty devising regulations to achieve this end. Furthermore, the legal precedents to date suggest that the federal courts will be more stringent in applying the Fourteenth Amendment to voucher systems than to neighborhood school systems. The courts have repeatedly thrown out voucher systems designed to maintain segregation, whereas they have shown no such general willingness to ban the neighborhood school. Outside the South, then, those who believe in integration may actually have an easier time achieving this goal with voucher systems than they will with the existing public school system. Certainly, the average black parent's access to integrated schools would be increased under a voucher system of the kind proposed by the Center. Black parents could apply to any school in the

5 Andrew Greeley and Peter Rossi. *The Education of Catholic Americans*. Chicago: Aldine, 1966.

system, and the proportion of blacks admitted would have to be at least equal to the proportion who applied. This gives the average black parent a far better chance of having their children attend an integrated school than at present. There is, of course, no way to compel black parents to take advantage of this opportunity by actually applying to schools that enroll whites. But the opportunity would be there for all.

The Proposed Demonstration The voucher plan described above could in theory be adopted by any local or state jurisdiction interested in increasing diversity in schools and parental choice in selection of schools. In the long run it is not much more expensive than the present system. But the Center has recommended to OEO that a demonstration project be financed first, carefully regulated to ensure that the proposed rules are followed, and carefully monitored to test the effects of dispensing public education funds in the form of vouchers. The Center has recommended that at least 10,000 elementary school students be included in the demonstration site, and that the demonstration city (or part of a city) should contain a population which is racially and economically heterogeneous. Ideally some alternative schools should already exist in the selected area, and the prospects for beginning other new schools should be reasonable.

In March, 1970, staff and consultants of the Center embarked on an extensive investigation of the feasibility of conducting a demonstration project. Superintendents of schools in all cities with a population in excess of 150,000 in the 1960 census, which were not under court or administrative order to desegregate their school systems, were contacted by mail. Expressions of interest were followed up. Meetings were held in interested cities around the country. Local and state school administrators were contacted, as were interested school officials, teachers' groups, parents' organizations, and nonpublic schools.

As of November 1, 1970, five communities had decided to apply for preliminary planning funds. If one or more of these cities decides to conduct a demonstration of the voucher program, we may have a chance at last to test what contributions a voucher program could make to improving the quality of education available to children in this country. If, on the other hand, the National Education Association and the American Federation of Teachers have their way, we shall have no test at all.

Reslicing the School Pie

The writers are all lawyers and the authors of
Private Wealth and Public Education (1970),
published by Harvard University Press. Mr.
Coons is professor of law at the University of
California, Berkeley; Mr. Sugarman is an
associate with O'Melveny and Myers,
Los Angeles; and Mr. Clune is a member of
the Illinois Bar and Legal Counsel and research
associate at the Illinois Institute for Social Policy.
In this essay, the writers focus on alternative
regulated voucher systems that permit a
family to choose not only a type of school
but also the quality of school it desires. In
addition to the authors' book, a discussion of
the issues raised by unequal allocation
of funds among school districts can be
found in *The Quality of Inequality*,
Charles U. Daly, ed. (1968).

John E. Coons, Stephen D. Sugarman, and William H. Clune III, "Reslicing the School Pie,"
Teachers College Record, *Vol. 72, No. 4 (May 1971), pp. 485-493.*

John E. Coons
Stephen D. Sugarman
William H. Clune III

State systems of taxing and spending for elementary and secondary education tend to combine misery and mystery in equal parts. Historically, the school money debates have been dominated by specialists on such complex questions as "subvention," "overburden," and "equalization formulas," effectively insulating the institution from the scrutiny of its victims. Today, however, in what may be the last shot in the skirmish on poverty, school finance is finally receiving serious public attention:

ITEM. President Nixon has appointed a School Finance Commission. ITEM. The Supreme Court has twice in the past two years been asked to strike down as unconstitutional the methods by which public education is presently financed; it has not foreclosed the question, and may be forced to face the issue directly in its next term. ITEM. Governor Milliken of Michigan has proposed shifting from a shared state-local school finance arrangement to an essentially state funded one. ITEM. The Office of Economic Opportunity has announced its willingness to sponsor experimental tuition voucher programs; Governor Reagan of California has commented favorably on one form of the voucher plan. ITEM. Governor Rockefeller of New York has appointed a blue-ribbon commission to make a comprehensive examination of the quality, cost, and financing of elementary and secondary education for the coming decade.

All this may stimulate a large yawn; yet there may be surprises in store. A variety of hostile forces are beginning to converge on the old system. Lawyers, educators, and social scientists increasingly score the unfairness to students and taxpayers of our reliance upon local property taxes; voters (allegedly property owners) reject local bond issues, budgets, and property tax overrides at an alarming rate; striking teachers demand an even higher priority for education on our list of national commitments; school districts reluctantly shorten the school year because of the money pinch; Catholic schools either close or stagger along, praying with their public counterparts for a governmental rescue that will keep parochial pupils from landing in the overburdened public schools.

Ironically, this tumult comes as leading educational critics proclaim the utter irrelevance of current schooling, especially in our cities. The system is not diseased, they say; it is a corpse that more cash will simply cosmetize. Their hope —if hope they have—is integration, is accountability of teachers, is individualization or technology; it is not money. Even many of the most radical structural reformers, decentralizers, and political participators decline to engage seriously the question of economic support for their enterprises. Their know-nothing attitude is, to an extent, pardonable; financial reform will not itself revitalize education, and its pursuit lacks the allure of public combat over more visible and glamorous objectives. Regrettably, it is a precondition to improvement of any sort whatsoever.

Villains and Victims   However, even the idea of financial reform in education is as confused as the rhetoric of equal opportunity that confounds the debate. Lest we sin ourselves, an initial clarification is indicated. The issue is not quantity. Even conceding the onus of guilt borne by a curmudgeon federal government, *the critical need in school finance is not simply for more money*. The fundamental evil of the present system is reliance upon *local property taxation of unevenly distributed property wealth*. This is not so complex a matter as sometimes it is made to appear. Simply put the tragedy involves two villains and two victims, all four of which typically inhabit school districts with low property wealth per pupil. The villains are higher tax rates for education and lower spending in schools; the victims are the children and those who bear the taxes for their public schools.

Consider this example from Los Angeles County in California. Michael, a fifth grader, lives in the Walnut elementary district; in 1968-69 the cost of his public education was $500. His friend, Robert, lives in the Keppel elementary district; in that same year his fifth grade spent $786 per pupil. Each boy's family has the same income and owns a home of the same value (market and assessed). Michael's house is taxed at 3.28 percent of assessed valuation; Robert's at 2.33 percent. The California "system" thus provides substantially fewer school dollars for the children of those in the Walnut district who pay the higher tax rate. The example chosen is conservative. It is typical of our states.

Disaster of Form   The historical parent of this prodigy is the rough compromise that emerged from the struggle after 1850 between the public school enthusiasts and their individualist opponents. The victory of the schoolmen was never complete; education was made compulsory and universal, but the principle of state responsibility was never clearly

accepted. Instead, the local community became the foundation of "public" education, a result which tempered individualist fears of a monolith, making the
enterprise politically possible. In an agrarian economy with a fairly uniform
distribution of wealth within most states, this parceling out to local units of the
new duty to educate might have been seen as tolerable to both sides. After another quarter century of economic change, the nightmarish reality began to
surface. What the individualist had surrendered in the establishment of public
education was beyond recall; what the reformers had bargained for in equality
had become a casualty of the industrial revolution.

By 1900, the clustering of wealth in urban foci already was well under way.
Then, as now, school districts in most states depended for their principal support upon the power delegated to them to tax the value of real property located
within their boundaries. As the disparities in taxable wealth widened among
communities, education prospered in some districts and foundered in others
for reasons unrelated either to local need or local enthusiasm. Balkanization of
education had come to mean good schools in the rich cities and the virtual col-
lapse of many rural districts. Public education has never recovered from this
original disaster of form. The identity of rich and poor districts shifts and
changes with time; in some cases cities favored through the first half of this
century may now face the problem of corporate poverty. But for town and
country alike the iron rule of the system is unaltered: the dollars spent for a
child's education are a function of the wealth of his school district. Today in
some states the taxable wealth per pupil in the richest districts is 100 times the
wealth in the poorest.

State "equalization" programs of aid to poor districts have been the typical
twentieth century response to this problem. From state to state there is considerable variation in these devices whose details are impenetrable to the amateur
and deserve no attention here. Their principal effect is anesthesia for the out-
rage of the victims. State support for poor districts is made highly visible and
thus politically effective in tranquilizing local indignation. However, the notion
that the districts have been "equalized" is transcendent fiction. So far from
reality is it that in California, Wisconsin, Illinois, and elsewhere millions in
"state aid" have been identified which, under existing legislation, actually benefit only the wealthy districts. This aid is a bonus for being rich! The consequence of the system is disparity in spending, which in California districts
ranges from well below $500 to $3,000 per pupil.

Seeing this helps to explain the durability of the local property tax despite
the predictions and imprecations of politicians, property owners, journalists,
and others prone to discover taxpayer revolts. Plainly, it survives because it is
the basis of a highly effective system of privilege. Communities that enjoy high
property values per pupil, either because of the presence of wealthy residents

or of industry, can have good schools (and other municipal services) for a cheaper tax rate than their poorer neighbors. Such communities and their residents have a strong interest in preserving the discrimination.

The benefited class is a peculiar one: it is not distinguished simply by personal wealth. Rich families sometimes live in districts poor in taxable wealth, while some of the richest districts are industrial enclaves inhabited largely by blue collar or poor families. Overall, however, there appears to be a correlation between personal wealth and district wealth, and it is the children of the poor living in poor districts who are the most poignant victims. These families cannot afford to move or to choose private schools. By and large they are white families, at least in the North. Minorities tend to cluster in larger cities near or somewhat above average in wealth. This is not to say that such minority children are never victims of fiscal discrimination *inside* their district of residence, though that particular swindle itself is beginning to decline.

The problem, then, is not vicious motivation or conspiratorial purposes, but merely wild and arbitrary imposition of privilege and deprivation according to the accident of district wealth. The evil is blindly structural in the most primitive sense that the state has created a discrimination machine. Districts above the median in wealth naturally resist change, and they are politically vigorous; districts of roughly average wealth have no clear stake in reform and are apathetic or even turned off by the centralist rhetoric of most of the reformers. Only poor districts would clearly benefit, and their historic failure to move the legislatures is not surprising.

Judicial Intervention   Ironically, this chronic political impotence of the victims itself may assist reform by sanctioning judicial intervention. It is not fanciful to describe the projected relief for children of poor districts as another rescue of a (literally) disenfranchised minority. Who but the Supreme Court could brake this machine so insulated from ordinary majoritarian politics?

However, seen as a constitutional issue for the court under the Equal Protection guarantee, the matter becomes complex. Three pointed problems of judicial role threaten to bar even threshold examination of the problem. First, to be effective in dealing with any issue of this magnitude, the Court must be able to articulate a clear and principled basis for condemning the system. The principle must permit reasonably accurate prediction of future decisions involving a variety of possible legislative responses. Second, sensitive to its nonelective and antimajoritarian character, the Court should shrink from imposing a uniform system upon the states. Its primary objective should be not to bind but to loose the legislatures from the existing log jam, sparing whatever is tolerable in the old order and permitting a wide variety of new state systems. Third, the

Court will need confidence that its will can be enforced. However, the first is the key to all; the primary concern must be the discovery of a satisfactory standard by which to judge state systems. So far it is the failure of litigants to offer such a standard that has alienated the judges who have spoken on the issue.

Until this year two cases had reached the Supreme Court, one each from Illinois and Virginia. The three-judge federal panel in Illinois dismissed for lack of "discoverable and manageable standards" a suit which asserted a duty of the state under the 14th Amendment to spend for each child according to his individual needs. The Supreme Court affirmed without argument or opinion, and with but one dissent. Except for an additional dissent a similar complaint in the Virginia case met an identical fate in the following term of the high Court. Counsel in the several remaining cases are seeking a standard that will pass judicial muster and yet be effective. The problem is urgent, as crucial cases in California and elsewhere proceed to their final disposition. Thus far, the Court appears to have kept an open mind. A recent appeal in a school finance case from Florida presented an opportunity to seal off debate on the issue. Instead, the Court sent the case back for trial. This leaves the final judicial answer perhaps a year or more away.

The difficulty in this quest for principle is illustrated by the disunity of the critics, some of whose proposals have bordered on the extreme. For example, one formula—an analogy to the one man-one vote rule—asserts a duty to spend equal dollars per child throughout the state. The federal judges in the Illinois suit declared this "the only possible standard" and then rejected it. Only die-hard egalitarians would quarrel with the court's assertion that a rule forbidding compensatory spending is the last thing we need. What then of the "needs" formula proposed by the Illinois and Virginia complaints? The primary flaw in such a standard is that it is really not a standard at all; indeed, it is the replacement of all standards by the purest nominalism, each child bearing his own "rule." This approach may be satisfactory for educational philosophers; its appeal to judges is less obvious. Finding and enforcing the dollar rights of each child according to his needs (whatever that may mean) is not an activity in which courts will be eager to engage.

Two other formulas contending for scholarly and judicial attention at least can claim status as bona fide principles. Each is simple and is cast in the negative—that is, as a proscription of particular state action, thus avoiding the problems raised by insisting upon a duty of specific legislative behavior. Under *Proposition One* the state would merely be forbidden to permit variations in district or family wealth to affect spending per pupil. *Proposition Two* would agree but would add a prohibition against variations in the number of dollars spent on any child by virtue of his place of residence. This difference is highly significant. *Proposition Two* (Professor Arthur Wise) is a centralizing prin-

ciple satisfied only by statewide standards for spending. *Proposition One*
would permit local decision resulting in the spending of more or fewer dollars
per pupil from one unit to another, so long as those variations in spending are
not in any degree the consequence of variations in wealth.

Together these two propositions draw the line of battle between the centralists and those favoring local incentive. The former are outraged that the
quality of education could be affected by differing enthusiasm for education
from district to district. On the other hand, the latter see in local decision a
source of health, variety, and citizen involvement plus an insurance against the
statewide mediocrity risked by centralization. In any case, one's policy preference in this regard should not be confounded with his view of the Constitution. Even centralizers should prefer *Proposition One* if the Court sees preservation of local choice as the condition of its intervention. Continued local choice,
liberated from the effects of wealth variations, is a more attractive prospect
than no reform at all; besides, who can say the legislatures will not be persuaded
to centralize once the old order is invalidated under *Proposition One?*

Power Equalizing: Districts   However, our own
preference for *Proposition One* is not purely tactical. The use of relatively
small units to determine important aspects of educational policy seems to us
plausible; and it is quite feasible to make existing school districts substantially
equal in their power to raise money for education. Even retaining the property
tax as the local source (we would prefer a local income tax), such parity of
power could be managed through a combination of state subsidies, redistrict-
ing, and other devices. The resulting system is called "power equalizing." Suppose, for example, the legislature provided that all districts might tax local real
property at a rate of from 1 percent to 3 percent and that the district's own
choice of specific tax level within that range would, in accord with a relation
set by law, fix the district's spending level. The amount per pupil actually
raised by the tax would be irrelevant. What would count is how hard the district chose to tax itself, not the wealth on which the tax was levied. The relation might be as simple as the following table:

Locally Chosen Tax	Permitted Spending Per Student
1% (minimum permitted)	$ 500
1.1%	550
2%	1,000
3% (maximum permitted)	1,500

Mechanically it might operate in a variety of ways. For example, if a district
taxing at 2 percent raised $800 per student, it would be subsidized $200 per
student from general sources by the state. If a district were wealthier and raised

$1,200 at 2 percent, $200 of this would be redistributed as part of the subsidy for poorer districts. Alternatively all proceeds of the locally chosen taxes could be paid into a state pool with all disbursements made from that pool based solely upon the local tax rate.

Power equalizing formulas can be adjusted to take into account variations in the cost of educational goods and services from place to place. They can also be tuned to reflect subtler economic factors such as municipal overburden and educational considerations such as the "needs" of disadvantaged (or, for that matter, gifted) students. In short, power equalizing formulas provide the base for any true "compensatory" scheme.

Power equalizing also is an answer to the central dilemma of the community control movement: how can an urban enclave like Ocean Hill-Brownsville achieve political autonomy without accepting economic prostration? Every district, irrespective of size or wealth, through power equalizing can be rendered both independent and equal in the power to educate its children. The poverty of a neighborhood's tax resources cannot by itself justify continued subordination to a larger school district. If the state desires it, Ocean Hill-Brownsville can be economically as unfettered as Scarsdale.

Power Equalizing: Families Some have suggested that power equalizing can satisfy both the centralist drive for equality and the objectives of local government by a further extension to the family level. Imagine, for example, that each family with school-age children is a small school district that has been equalized in its power to tax itself and to spend for education. All parents would choose among schools, each of which operates at a set level of cost per pupil, say $500, $800, $1,100, and $1,400. The school would receive its income (for secular instruction) from the state; it could charge no further tuition. The family's choice of a school cost level would fix the rate of a special tax upon its own income. The tax rates also would vary by family income class with the aim of equalizing for all families the economic sacrifice required to attend any school at a given spending level. For example, a welfare mother might pay $15 in tax for all her children to attend a $500 school; for that same school the tax price to a middle-class family might approach the full $500 cost, while the price to a rich family would exceed the full cost. A $1,400 school might cost these same three families $100, $1,000, and $2,000 respectively.

Schools in such a system could be all public, all private, or mixed. The constraints on curriculum could be few or many, but any substantial limitation would frustrate at least some of the purposes for trying such a system in the first place. One important object is, after all, for the first time to give a true choice to all families—including the poor. Through family choice, it is argued,

competition and experimentation would be stimulated and variety and quality thereby enhanced. Also better matching of schools and children would be
effected by the judgments of parents and children than by an impersonal attendance boundary for the neighborhood or the judgment of an expert. In providing choice to the parent, an answer also would be given to the other dilemma
in the community control movement: how to maintain a true "community"
while respecting the interests of dissenting minorities. In a family based system,
the community would be transformed from an artificial and inescapable community of geography to a community of interests, one freely chosen and freely
abandoned.

Obviously the details of such a system would have to be carefully
tailored if such ancillary policies as racial integration, fair competition, minimum standards, and job security for teachers were to be satisfied. The model
"Family Choice in Education Act" which has been drafted to express these
policies comprises hundreds of provisions. It encourages private schools with
guaranteed loans but protects public schools against unfair competition by
limiting the capitalization of private schools. For similar reasons it disallows
contributions either from interested sources or for ideological objectives. The
model act also puts pupil admission to a school on a random basis, thereby maximizing racial and social integration. To assist the choices of schools by parents,
an elaborate system of information and counseling would be provided. Of
course, free and adequate transport would have to be made available. In
all respects, the complex provisions of the model act strive to assure the fullest
measure of independent action and equality of opportunity for schools, parents, and pupils.

However, an interesting division recently has emerged between what may be
viewed as the centralists and decentralists among family choice proponents.
The schism is illustrated by a proposal for educational vouchers outlined by the
Center for the Study of Public Policy at Cambridge, a proposal that conceiv-
ably will be supported by the Office of Economic Opportunity in a series of
experiments. (*Teachers College Record*, February, 1971.) Though reflecting
some of the aims of the model family choice act, the CSPP proposal specifically
rejects it and offers in its place a striking contrast. Rather than provide equal
access for all to schools of different quality, the CSPP model deliberately tends
to equalize all schools in the voucher system at a level of quality to be centrally,
not parentally, determined. This uniformity would be achieved by giving more
money to schools with a higher population of disadvantaged children. It
would not allow for variation in spending in accord with the tax effort families
are willing to make for their education. Effectively, parents who are poor
would be denied the opportunity to aspire to an education which is not merely

different in style but qualitatively superior to the governmentally mandated minimum.

The CSPP model is the expression of a plausible—if, to us, mistaken—value choice in education. It is probably compatible with the constitutional test we have offered, since (depending upon its eventual details) it divorces quality in public education from variations in wealth. Along with power equalizing systems—both district and family—it nicely illustrates the boundless possibilities for experiment and change in the structure of American education. If the old order survives another century, it will not be for want of alternative models.

PART III
Vouchers: Pro and Con

The Peaceful Uses of
Education Vouchers

Stephen Arons is a member of the Massachusetts
Bar and a Fellow Staff Attorney at the
Center for the Study of Public Policy. In
this essay, Mr. Arons, who was a member of
the CSPP team, looks at proposals for
regulated vouchers from a wide range of
practical, legal, and political perspectives.

Stephen Arons, "Equity, Option, and Vouchers," Teachers College Record, *Vol. 72, No. 3
(February 1971), pp. 337-363.*

Stephen Arons

Adam Smith, Tom Paine, Milton Friedman, and Christopher Jencks are hardly peas in a political pod. Yet these intellectually astute gentlemen may be found united in the name of "education vouchers."

About the time of the first American Revolution, Adam Smith suggested that the state limit its support of schooling to capital expenses, leaving parents to pay the schoolmaster's salary if they were satisfied with his performance.[1] The idea was to preserve a competitive market for schooling. It was left to Tom Paine, whom Smith attacked vigorously for his political views, to work out a detailed plan of tax rebates which the poor could use on their children's education.[2] Two centuries later economist Milton Friedman suggested that all parents of school age children be given a flat grant voucher to be used at "approved" schools.[3] The idea was to reduce government intervention in education and return to what was by then a long-lost competitive market in schooling. This time around it was left to Christopher Jencks and company, under a contract from the Office of Economic Opportunity, to provide a comprehensive study of economically redistributive vouchers as a means of financing compulsory schooling.[4]

The current rebirth of discussion, research, and rancor over the subject is, in part, occasioned by the federal government's interest in experimenting with some form of the simple idea of giving parents vouchers with which they may "pay" for their child's education at the school of their choice. The idea has also found expression in the draft of a statute designed to eliminate the dependence

1   Adam Smith. *The Wealth of Nations.* London, England: W. Strahan and T. Cadell, 1778.
2   The idea probably appeared first in Thomas Paine's *The Rights of Man.* A brief discussion of it can be found in E. G. West, "Tom Paine's Voucher Scheme for Public Education," *Southern Economic Journal*, Vol. 33, 1966-67, p. 378.
3   Milton Friedman. *Capitalism and Freedom.* Chicago: University of Chicago Press, 1969.
4   The initial OEO report, "Education Vouchers," was compiled by Christopher Jencks and colleagues. It is available from the Center for the Study of Public Education, 58 Boylston St., Cambridge, Massachusetts 02138. The report is a feasibility study which looks toward a joint federal-local experiment with vouchers.

of school quality upon district wealth,[5] five attempts by Southern states to avoid court-ordered desegregation,[6] several proposed forms of "parochaid."[7] the expressed desires of a few alternative schools, and proposals for performance contracting in Texas and California.[8] Almost everybody seems to have his finger in it someplace. Professor John Coons, who is one of the most sophisticated analysts of the legal and economic aspects of voucher plans, offers the political observation that his "family power equalizing plan" should be ". . . attractive to Black Panthers, John Birchers, Muslims, Catholics (laymen not clerics), classical liberals, education experimenters, property owners, residents of poor districts, and other disparate and overlapping cadres."[9]

When all these people are reported to agree with a political scheme, one wonders whether we have reached the millenium (there is no corroborating evidence for this), or whether the slogan "education vouchers," like "law and order" or "guaranteed adequate income," tends to obscure the ideological and practical differences among us.

The groups who do or might support vouchers are perhaps able to agree because they focus on very different aspects of the idea. For example, in one camp it is a means of rationalizing the tax structure and eliminating economic discrimination in resource allocation for schooling. Elsewhere, it is a means of breaking up the majoritarian monopoly over public schools and supporting

5 Professor John Coons of Berkeley Law School is currently working on a redraft of a voucher scheme for California. The statute is designed to comply with the constitutional principle advanced by Professor Coons and his colleagues that the quality of public education may not be a function of wealth other than the wealth of the state as a whole. A lucid explication of this principle can be found in John E. Coons, William H. Clune III, and Stephen D. Sugarman. *Private Wealth and Public Education*. Cambridge, Mass.: Harvard University Press, 1970.

6 The Federal courts have turned back attempts by Louisiana, Virginia, Alabama, South Carolina, and North Carolina to avoid court ordered desegregation through the establishment of voucher plans devoid of protections against discrimination. See, *Griffin v. State Board of Education*, 296 F. Supp. 565 (E.D. Vir., 1969); *Poindexter v. Louisiana Financial Assistance Commission*, 296 F. Supp. 686 (E.D.La., 1968), aff'd. per curiam, 393 U.S. 17 (1968); *Lee v. Macon County Board of Education*, 267 F. Supp. 458 (M.D.Ala., 1967); *Brown v. South Carolina State Board of Education*, 296 F. Supp. 199 (D.S.C., 1968), aff'd per curiam, 393 U.S. 222 (1968); *Hawkins v. North Carolina Board of Education*, 11 Race Rel. L. Rep. 745 (W.D.N.C., 1966).

7 Per capita grants or vouchers for private schools have been proposed in Illinois, Missouri, Wisconsin, and Iowa in the last two years. The term "parochaid" is derived from the primary beneficiaries of this legislation.

8 In 1969, a bill in the California legislature (A.B. 2118) would have provided a one thousand dollar voucher to parents of children in poor districts attending schools which fell below certain minimum standards. The use of the vouchers would have been tied to a performance contracting system requiring the alternative provider of educational services to guarantee student progress.

9 John Coons, "Recreating the Family's Role in Education," *Inequality in Education*, Nos. 3 & 4. Publication of the Harvard Center for Law and Education.

a more diverse system of education. These two points of view may never intersect. The tax experts may not care whether the schools are operated by a publicly elected authority or by independent corporations; and the diversifiers may address themselves to diversity, while giving no thought to the economic consequences or burdens of a voucher scheme. As a result, a good deal of the potential agreement may stem from the isolated nature of each group's interests. Indeed, this would be an expected attitude for those supporting a system based on a modified form of free enterprise—let each man look after his own interests.

Ironically enough, what these diverse groups do share is the desire to bring about structural rather than particularistic school reform. Whereas school reform used to be bottomed in complaints against classroom overcrowding, inadequate texts, and the production of more technocrats to compete with the makers of Sputnik, we are now dealing with more basic structural changes, such as parent control, equitable allocation of resources, and decentralization. From a system-wide perspective, however, merely adjusting the interests of these disparate groups—especially when these groups have vastly different levels of political power reflecting social and political discrimination or oppression—is not likely to yield an equitable system of schooling. It is necessary to view a voucher plan as a systematic political restructuring of schooling, rather than simply as another pie to be carved up by existing interest groups, if we are to feel any confidence at all that vouchers will create the objective conditions for solving school problems instead of being simply a reflection of the existing inequities and inhumanities of public schooling.

To discuss these inequities and inhumanities at length is not the purpose of this essay. Suffice it to say that the structural reforms which are now being demanded on all sides arise from the enormous gap between the promise of public schooling and its performance—a gap which has grown to proportions which prompt the sensible person to wonder whether we are not using the wrong political system altogether for the governance and provision of public education. The common school promises to be the melting pot wherein all have an equal opportunity to gain the prerequisites of a fruitful life; but the evidence increases that not only do the schools discriminate against the poor, the black, the Indians, the Chicanos, the sensitive, and the creative, but they have never significantly helped any minority group.[10] Is the public school the place where people of all backgrounds gather and share in the public decisions about education? The upper-middle-class and those with institutional religious affiliations continue to leave the public school, buying their way out of the majority

---

10 For a discussion of the historical inaccuracies in the assumption that public schools have been an important source of upward mobility, *see*, Colin Greer, "Public Schools: The Myth of the Melting Pot," *Saturday Review*, November 15, 1969.

decision and leaving the rest behind. Is the public school so dependent upon the approval of all groups that it serves them all equally adequately? The schools' responsiveness to the different needs of their pupils has generally been a tracking system which locks students into limited futures and whose deleterious effects are only beginning to surface.[11] Are the public schools the very expression of Dewey's philosophy of child-centered learning? The schools are so overburdened by managerial goals that it is nearly impossible for a humanist to survive there.[12] The list of goals held by the public and broken by the public schools goes on and on. But running between the lines of this list is a single nagging question: Is the political structure of schooling incapable of being used to solve these problems? To those who advocate the use of vouchers, the answer is yes.

Whether vouchers will, in fact, be an improvement is a speculative question. It can be approached initially by analyzing a series of issues—economic model, admissions policies, accountability, the range of alternatives, and church-state separation.[13] The attempt here will be to point out some of the value decisions which are imbedded in each major issue.

The basis of the educational voucher system is the channeling of public education funds through the families of school age children. Schools which are eligible for public aid receive that aid by attracting students who bring with them vouchers which can be cashed in with the state or local government. The funds are public, and this constitutes the first element of the definition of public schools; but the use of the funds is not restricted to schools operated by public agencies. This part of the definition of public schools has been deleted. Since the entire system rests upon parental choice of schools, the first problem which arises concerns the value of the vouchers and their relationship to the wealth of parents.

The Economic Framework   At present, public schools are supported by a combination of tax monies collected by state and local governments and relatively small categorical grants from the federal government, mostly under Title I of the Elementary and Secondary Education Act. The local share is generally the largest and is extremely retrogressive, since it is based on *ad valorem* property taxes. All of this revenue is paid into

---

11 About the best short discussion of the tracking problem is Em Hall, "The Road to Educational Failure," *Inequality in Education*, No. 5. Publication of the Harvard Center for Law and Education.

12 The operative irrelevance of humanism in public schools is not likely to change under present political circumstances. *See*, Thomas Green, "Schools and Communities: A Look Forward," *Harvard Educational Review*, Vol. 39, No. 2, 1969.

13 These topics are based on the structure of the OEO interim report in which the author participated.

a school fund, the distribution of which is directly under the control of the local board of education. This money is allocated on functional and school-by-school bases in accordance with budget requests which wend their way through the school bureaucracy. The voucher scheme turns this system upside down, collecting the taxes centrally but dispersing them immediately and completely to parents—individual consumers whose choice of schools determines which schools shall be funded. The director of the school must look to his clientele rather than to a central bureaucracy for his funds. He operates his school in a basically decentralized framework, making his own decisions on use of funds and being accountable to parents of his students within the basic constitutional and policy constraints of the plan.

Several economic models have been advanced which vary according to how the value of the voucher is determined and whether individual parents may supplement vouchers.[14] The voucher system creates a regulated market in which schools compete for students, and students try to enroll in schools they find most in line with their needs. If such a situation is to avoid becoming mired in the discrimination and degradation which characterize so much of the competitive market for consumer goods, it is essential that every family come to the marketplace with something like equal resources. This principle effectively eliminates plans which allow parents to supplement their vouchers with private funds. To allow such supplementation would exacerbate existing wealth disparities, and put the poor and lower-middle-class majority at a competitive disadvantage in buying adequate education. Moreover, the ability to supplement by even $200 would have the effect of splitting the middle class off from the poor. Beyond this restriction on supplementation there are three ways in which a redistributive or compensatory goal can be attained in fixing the voucher value.

(1) Perhaps the simplest way to provide equal bargaining power would be to fix the value of the vouchers at the same level for everyone and prohibit schools from charging more. This model, however, does not respond to the argument that it costs more to provide the same resources for "disadvantaged" youth than for advantaged youth. Neither does it allow any variations in school expenditure levels responsive to the desires and priorities of the parents. It also leaves to the political process, presumably on the state level, the decision to raise the level of spending in public education.

(2) Another method of equalizing all families' bargaining power within the voucher system would be to assign values to the vouchers in inverse proportion to family wealth. Thus a family with a $2,000 annual income might get a

---

14 A number of possible economic models are dealt with in the OEO report, including some not mentioned here: the compulsory private scholarship model and the achievement model.

$1,500 voucher for each child, and a family with a $20,000 annual income might get only $150 per child, with gradations in between. Voucher schools would have maximum tuition limits set by the state, and supplementation by well-to-do families would not be allowed to exceed these limits (for example, it might be a $750 per year limit, requiring the $20,000 family to contribute $600 of its resources while rewarding the school with a $750 windfall for enrolling the low-income child). This plan is subject to further variations, the most interesting of which is to prevent the value of the voucher from dropping below the maximum tuition rate even for well-to-do parents, provided that they send their children to publicly managed schools. The aim here would be to induce these parents to use publicly operated schools. For example:

If Your Income Is:	Your Voucher Might Be Worth:	
	In a Public School	In a Nonpublic Voucher School
0–2,000	$1,500	$1,500
2,001–4,000	1,300	1,300
4,001–6,000	1,000	1,000
6,001–7,600	750	750
7,601–9,000	750	650
9,001–11,000	750	500
11,001–15,000	750	250
15,001–20,000	750	150
Over 20,000	750	0

One of the flaws in the income-inverse (regulated compensatory) model is that it fixes school expenditures at a single level and leaves no room for variations dependent upon the priority which the individual attaches to institutionalized, formalized education. To many people, a school's managed environment and packaged teaching are not conducive to real learning, even if they are responsive to some concepts of teaching. For those who do not equate compulsory attendance with educational opportunity, it makes sense to provide the possibility of varying levels and kinds of education. It is likely that such variation would result in different costs for schooling, something not provided for in this economic model.

The income-inverse model also disregards the fact that low-income children may not necessarily be harder or more expensive to educate. It has been observed that the same services often cost more in ghetto schools than elsewhere because teachers are reluctant to work in ghettos. Unless a child is suffering from a physical or perceptual handicap, however, this explanation for increased cost of educating the disadvantaged is based as much on teacher attitudes and characteristics as student handicaps. The problems are relational, not simply a matter of a student's inadequacy. A number of community schools are discovering that excellent education can be provided in poor communities at average cost. Under a more open system the increased costs of educating disadvantaged youth might evaporate.

Another way of equalizing would be to assess by a need index whether a particular child is "disadvantaged," and to compensate him for this by increasing the value of his voucher. Essentially this is a means of making his presence in a school more desirable because he is worth more money to the school. Secondly, it serves to help the school pay for the supposedly increased cost of educating such a disadvantaged child.[15] Its basis of equalizing is not income level, but educational disadvantage, though the two are often correlated. The judgments which would have to be made here, except when they involve physiological handicaps, seem difficult if not impossible,[16] involving as they do some single or highly limited standard of educability (implying certain goals of education probably not shared by all and definitely antithetical to the voucher principle of fostering diversity in education). Even if one were to accept an unidimensional standard, the state of knowledge about causes and effects in schooling seems modest enough to warrant severe skepticism about the practicability of such a plan. Most important, perhaps, a system which assumes that personal growth is measurable is likely to be insulting and damaging on a grand scale.

A third model, advanced by Professor Coons at Berkeley, responds to the desire to have different levels of school expenditures dependent upon the priorities of parents. Professor Coons's "family power equalizing plan" applies to the decision on voucher value the same principle of diversity which undergirds the whole voucher idea. All previous plans required that the value of the vouchers be set by the political process—a majoritarian decision about either the flat rate available to all families and charged by schools or the compensatory needs of children. Coons's plan makes the tuition amount and the individual parents' sacrifice dependent upon the parents' decision; and makes the overall education tax rate dependent on the sum of such individual decisions. That is, it changes the locus of decision-making from legislature to family not only

15 This point raises again the question of whether it is or need be more expensive to educate disadvantaged children. It should be noted that under this plan even though the school receives extra funds because it enrolls disadvantaged children the money received could be spread out and spent on all the school's students. Remedying this would require regulations similar to but more effective than those adopted for Title I of ESEA.

16 Two attempts at convincing the courts that need criteria can be a workable standard for judging the constitutional adequacy of school resources have failed, *McInnis v. Ogilvie*, 384 U.S. 383 (1969) and *Burruss v. Wilkerson*, 301 F. Supp. 1237 (1968).

with regard to which schools shall be attended and supported, but at what level and at what individual cost. To make it all more complicated and seemingly magical, this is done within the bounds of a redistributive taxing formula. A general idea of how such a scheme would work can be given by suggesting what decisions the parent faces.

Each school which wanted to receive vouchers would decide at which of four tuition levels it would operate (e.g., $500, $800, $1,100, $1,700). Each parent might then receive a graph on which he could locate his adjusted gross family income, the tuition level of the school which he wanted his child to attend, and the tax burden on him for that level. The cost to the parent (indicated on the graph) is calculated on the basis of a progressive tax schedule with adjustments for marginal utility affecting the tax effort of low income families. This cost is not a payment but a self-imposed tax. The entire tax system works off a state-wide income tax, and therefore, has a maximum redistributive effect.[17]

In looking at the graph, it may appear that family C with the $26,000 income is paying a self-tax of $1,250, but receiving a voucher worth only $1,100. The logical outcome of such an arrangement, were it in fact the way the scheme worked, would be that people whose incomes exceeded the breakeven point would not attend voucher schools, and that economic segregation would result. In reality, however, the point at which such a decision is economically desirable is much higher than the graph indicates. This is so for two reasons. First, the self-tax is a tax rather than a payment to a private school, and is therefore deductible from federal income taxes. This means that high-income families may, in fact, still be paying less than the voucher amount even when the graph shows a self-tax in excess of the voucher. Second, the self-tax does not increase for a family with more than one child. Family C can get two or three $1,100 vouchers for the same $1,250.[18]

The Coons model[19] for setting the value of vouchers on an individual basis (within the four tuition rates permitted) within a progressive tax structure attempts to equalize the *power* of each family to choose the resource level and school it desires. It is not a strict equalitarian system in the sense of providing every family with identical vouchers, but it does try to insure that differences which exist are based upon the values and preferences of the family rather than the accident of their wealth.[20]

17 It should be noted that a state's general revenues form part of the fund paying vouchers. Self-imposed education tax would not produce enough revenue in itself for all payments.
18 It has been suggested that this is ecologically unsound, even if it makes economic or political sense.
19 Coons, Clune, and Sugarman, *op. cit.*
20 There are of course other municipal services for which the poor must pay and which are not power equalized as education would be under this plan. The ability to attain

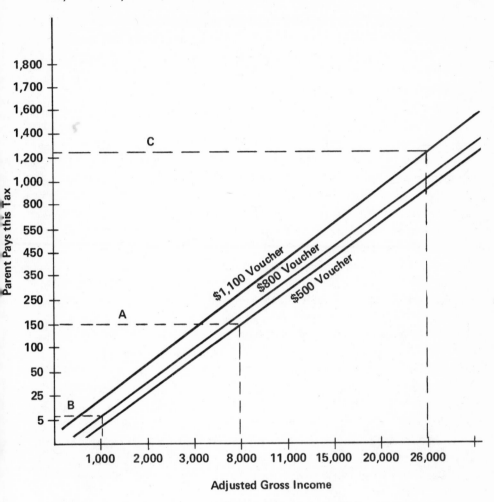

Family A — income $8,000 — wants $500 voucher — cost to them is $150
B — income $1,000 — wants $800 voucher — cost to them is $8.50
C — income $26,000 — wants $1,100 voucher — cost to them is $1,250

(Note: This graph is modeled after one being used by Professor Coons for his draft voucher statute. The figures are my own and do *not* reflect Professor Coons's research or design.)

It is for permitting variation in school expenditures that this model has been severely questioned. It is contended that those families which will make the smallest relative effort (i.e., choose the lowest self-tax) are the ones which value education least and are most in need of attending the best schools. This is

_____

adequate education and police protection, for example, is still skewed in favor of the middle and upper classes. The logical consequence of this line of thought is probably a radical equalizing of wealth throughout the country, or at least equalization of basic services.

entirely speculative, since there is little or no evidence that the distribution of low effort would correspond with high educational needs. In fact, a partial counterargument has been advanced stating that poor districts tend to make a greater tax effort relative to their resources than do wealthy school districts. Argument and counterargument hinge partly on correlations between income level and educational aspirations. The answer to the question is extremely important in determining whether the voucher scheme would tend to aggravate or alleviate segregation of disadvantaged children in schools. It remains a question, however, and is not likely to be resolved except by experimentation.

A second criticism of the Coons model is that public schools would feel constrained to charge the lowest possible tuition in order to maintain their images as free schools. The result of such a development would be that the publicly operated schools would be attended only by children whose parents attached a low priority to education; and that they would have to deal with these children with the lowest level of resources. If the premise of this argument is correct, then the conclusion is probably also correct. But several points make the problem more likely to be resolved experimentally than speculatively. To begin with, it is unclear why publicly operated schools would feel they had to operate on the lowest voucher level. Professor Coons's draft statute mandates the state school authority to operate schools at a number of different levels to compete with private schools. But even if this were not so, it is only a guess that publicly operated schools would choose low level operations. In addition, it is erroneous to think of the lowest voucher level as constituting a free education, while the others cost the parents money. In fact, the entire system is paid for by the state out of tax revenues, and even the lowest voucher level requires a small self-imposed tax of the parents. All voucher schools are free and public in the sense that they are supported by state revenues. But all voucher parents pay self-imposed education taxes.

Both of these criticisms are serious and need to be answered by experimentation, though it appears that the federal experiment will not use the Coons model and will, therefore, never move past the level of bald assertion on these two points. It is interesting, ideologically, that the first criticism reflects a distrust of parents to make intelligent choices about their children's schooling. On the one hand, the voucher system is touted as a bulwark of diversity and free choice; on the other, parents are being saved from their own value systems (even after "sacrifice" is equalized) by benevolent social planning. Some choices do, of course, have to be prohibited, especially those which result in unconstitutional deprivations of equal opportunity for the black community and the poor. It would be unfortunate, however, not to distinguish unconstitutional and intolerable consequences from questions of social policy and valid personal differences of priority. Fuzzing these two has led to overcontrol of preferences and inadequate enforcement of rights in the past.

A final word about differing preferences in education as reflected in choices about the value of vouchers. There is a cogent line of thought which holds that formalized and institutionalized education in buildings called schools is not the only or even the best form of education. Following this line, it has been urged that schooling be restricted to ten or fifteen hours a week of technical in-struction (e.g., reading skills, mathematics), and that students be given the re-sources to do other educational things, anywhere, anytime, the rest of the week. A low expenditure voucher school could easily run such a limited program. Who would find the parent who chose it for his child a danger to the society?

There are infinite modifications and adjustments which could be made in all the economic models outlined above, and there are probably just as many arguments pro and con. It does seem clear that a prerequisite of any plan is limitation of parents' ability to supplement the voucher, as well as limitation on the school's ability to charge tuition above the voucher level. Both these regulations would be necessary, though not sufficient, to insure that all parents had equal financial bargaining power in seeking schools for their children. Beyond this a redistributive effect and some incentive for economic and abil-ity mixing within voucher schools can be achieved through skewing voucher amounts according to educational need, income level, or income level and fam-ily effort. The choices among these three imply different values and rest in part upon questions which will not be answered without some form of experi-mentation with each system.

Admissions Policies Making public funds equal-ly available to all parents for their children's education is one part of the defini-tion of public schools. An equally important part is guaranteeing, especially in a system which supports both publicly and privately operated schools, equal access to all students. But balancing the need to prevent unconstitutional and unconscionable discrimination with the desirability of having schools and school programs which are responsive to the differing needs of students is ex-tremely difficult. Public school systems which have attempted this balancing have floundered either on excessive rigidity and unresponsiveness—the attempt to put all students in one mold—or on overbroad, irrational, and self-fulfilling classifications of students—the increasingly ugly practice of tracking. The tale of racial and economic discrimination established by law in the South or by exclusive suburban neighborhoods in the North is long and depressing.

The promise of a system of relatively autonomous schools supported by public funds in a competitive framework is in part to provide us with more diversity and responsiveness. The problem is to find ways of securing this di-versity without creating or allowing invidious discrimination. If a school can pick all its students from among the applicants, what will prevent racial dis-crimination? If a school can exercise no choice when it has a surplus of applicants, how do schools with different educational philosophies or talents or specialties manifest themselves? Several different methods have been suggested for regulating the matching of pupils and schools. Each must deal not only with the problem of student selection but also with transfer and dismissal of students.[21]

In evaluating the various plans which have been advanced for regulation of admissions, a basic principle should be to make as few policy decisions as possible centrally. Attempting to prescribe exactly which students with which characteristics should attend which schools balks the entire idea of enhancing parental choice and creating diversity. This principle would disqualify any quota system. One can imagine an enormous bureaucracy attempting to classify students and identify desirable and undesirable traits for the purposes of insuring that every school took its share of undesirables. If nothing else, this reductionist approach to human personality and learning is morally offensive. Its efficacy is also in doubt.

A full lottery among applicants for oversubscribed schools has also been suggested.[22] This system would go farthest toward maximizing parental choice. Each parent would select a number of schools to which they wanted to send their children, ranking the choices by preference. If the first-choice school had more applicants than preannounced places, a lottery among all its applicants would be held. Those who did not get admitted would drop down to their second choice where oversubscription would cause another lottery. Such a plan would insure that no school could discriminate against a student on the basis of his race, sex, or any other characteristic. It would also insure, however, that no school could select a student because he would make a special contribution or fit well with the school's offerings.

If parental choice is important to a free market fostering schools which feel some control over the nature of their programs, it is essential to providing genuine alternatives run by people who care about what they are doing. The 100 percent lottery sacrifices too much of this, especially at a time when there are increasing numbers of people starting their own experimental schools and conceiving of them as communities rather than factories. A substantial amount of selectivity is likely to take place simply in the way the school presents itself to prospective parents. But the personal nature of the joint school-parent decision about whether a child is suited to the school and the school is what the child really wants and needs is watered down too much by the total lottery.

The lottery concept does, however, provide the most reliable protection

---

21 A thoughtful discussion of these issues and the general problem of admissions policies can be found in the OEO voucher report.

22 This is the plan advanced in the California statute being worked on by Professor Coons.

against invidious discrimination. Merely outlawing such discrimination and relying on court or administrative investigation and enforcement would probably create an enforcement problem beyond comprehension, as anyone who has had experience with Title VI of the Civil Rights Act of 1964 or Title I of ESEA can testify. A good, though hardly ideal, solution to this dilemma is presented in the Education Vouchers report. In the case of oversubscription a school would be entitled to choose 50 percent of its students on whatever criteria it pleased, and would have to fill the other 50 percent by lot from among the remaining applicants. This seems to provide adequate protection against discrimination, while allowing the school to have considerable influence over its own destiny. In this plan, as in the complete lottery, provision would have to be made for persons already attending the school (and perhaps their siblings) to retain their places. No school would be allowed to turn someone away except through lottery. The 50 percent lottery, though it is a compromise, does seem workable. It might be especially effective if coupled with an economic model which provides incentives to schools to choose children with educational disadvantages.

Accountability Up to this point the issues of economic fairness and equal accessibility to schools have been put forward as the core of a workable definition of public education. A third element in the popular conception of public education is the notion of majority policy control of all publicly funded schools. Adding this element to the definition, however, obscures many issues. It implies that some voucher schools are public, and some private, even though the "private" schools would be public in some very basic ways and the "public" schools would be more independent than they are now. Voucher schools would, in fact, be neither entirely private nor public in the present sense of these words. Nevertheless, the issue of how voucher schools are to be controlled—to whom they are to be accountable—must be dealt with.

Most voucher schemes envision a diverse system of schools which are equally accessible to all students and supported totally by public funds collected according to people's ability to pay and desire or need for education. These schools may be run by public authorities on a state or local level, by private corporations, by neighborhood parent groups, by teachers' collectives, or by any group of persons with an idea for a school and the ability to attract students. The entire system operates on the basis of decentralized decision-making by schools which are by and large autonomous. The public monopoly over educational policy expressed through single boards of education is replaced by a number of boards of education which are accountable to the parents of the school's students.[23] Such accountability may take the form of direct parental control over school policy (if this is the basic form of the school) or may be restricted to control exercised through the parent's consumer choice of whether he and his voucher continue to support the school. Underlying the accountability based on consumer economic power or the particular structure chosen by a particular school would be a set of state-wide regulations expressing justifiable minimum standards. At present, states maintain minimum standards which apply to both public and private schools, but these would have to be modified for a voucher plan.

Beyond admissions and funding requirements, accountability guaranteed by state regulations of voucher schools would be of two broad types: consumer protection and minimum educational standards. Since the system attempts to maximize parental choice of schools within the bounds of equal educational opportunity, the provision of reliable information about schools is absolutely essential. Such information would make parents aware of what choices actually existed by describing those schools in a way which protected parents against fraud or false or misleading claims. To accomplish this a special agency, independent of schools, would collect and disseminate information about how schools spend their voucher money, what their teacher qualifications were, what the school's philosophy was, how well its students had done by a variety of standards important to parents, what the physical plant was like, who went to the school, etc. There might be attached to this a limitation on the amount which schools could spend on advertising above and beyond the mandated information system. The provision of such vital information should also be coupled with a system of counseling which parents could use to aid themselves in making school choices.

Perhaps the most sensitive issue in such a consumer information system is the power inherent in the type of information presented. The students who attend Summerhill may, for example, be healthy, creative, happy, self-actualizing people, but such things do not necessarily appear on standardized reading achievement tests. The issue really concerns the kind of consciousness which will be encouraged by the information presented to parents as "important." As it is with performance contracting, any agency with the power to set standards for the evaluation of education by legitimizing some information and ignoring other information is in the position to manipulate the expectations of parents. This fact may be the beginning of an argument for having more than one independent agency responsible for collecting and disseminating information. Certainly, it argues for diversifying the standards of judgment as much as the

---

23 The draft California statute mandates the state education board to operate a number of schools to compete with privately operated ones. Whether these publicly operated schools will be decentralized is left to the state to decide.

schools themselves are diversified. In this regard it seems essential that schools be judged not only by some minimum standards which apply to all, but by their own explicit and varying goals.[24] The danger in not applying such a set of standards is that a single index of success will be established and the perceptual base of diversity will be undercut.

The magnitude of this problem both in attaining a commitment to diversity, which would result in a balanced information system, and in discovering what inputs are related to what outputs is enormous politically and intellectually. It is worth noting, however, that essentially the same problem faces the public schools under the present political structure. The amount and reliability of information about what is happening in public schools and how well they are doing is so meager as to make one wonder whether political campaigning for school board elections doesn't amount to false and misleading advertising there too.

Any state which compels children between six and sixteen to attend school will, beyond insuring informed parental choice, set minimum educational standards from which no deviation will be tolerated. At present such standards exist in the vague state laws which apply to local school boards and which form the framework for the certification of private schools.[25] The rationale for this type of regulation is twofold. A child who is required to spend seven hours a day for ten years in a school building ought to be assured that this experience will be something more than mere incarceration or babysitting. From this point of view the child ought to be entitled to particular benefits or usable offerings of benefits. Certainly, the child is entitled not to be psychologically or intellectually damaged by his experience in school. From another point of view, it may be that parents will make choices for their children which will not only be damaging to the child (the dangerous area of paternalistic protection emerges here), but will also have adverse effects on other children or on the society as a whole. Protecting the general public from the adverse consequences of individual decisions generally comes under the heading of regulating "spillover effects" or "neighborhood effects."[26] The object is to ascertain when an individual's decision has so great and so negative an effect on a person not involved in making that decision that the state is entitled to intervene. An example frequently cited would require that every child be taught to read and write English at the tenth grade level, i.e., no parent could choose a school

---

24 A good argument for such a standard is presented in Donald Erickson. *Public Controls for Non-Public Schools*. Chicago: University of Chicago Press, 1969.

25 John Elson, "State Regulation of Non-public Schools: The Legal Framework," in Erickson, *op. cit.*

26 E. G. West. *Education and the State*. New York: Transatlantic, 1969.

which was not committed to providing such instruction, or no school which did not teach these skills could receive voucher money.

It doesn't seem particularly difficult, Marshall McLuhan to the contrary notwithstanding, to agree on the importance of reading and writing to the maintenance of a modern society. There are probably other skills, notably a facility with numbers and an understanding of governmental process, which would also command easy assent. Past this point things become fuzzy. Since the intervention technique used here is explicit state requirements rather than argument or even financial (and resistible) incentives, the discussion can become quite heated; and the decisions can result in uniformity, violations of personal values, and even repression. There are already some limitations in this form of intervention. It is clear that the state may not require that every child attend a publicly run school because the state's power "excludes any general power ... to standardize its children by forcing them to accept instruction from public teachers only."[27] The state may, however, make reasonable regulations of schools, and it is usually not until such regulation begins to infringe on individual religious freedoms by tending to establish religion that the court has actually been willing to invalidate a state regulation of a public school.[28] Between affirming individual liberty to choose any reasonable form of schooling and actually striking down restrictions on such liberty, there is a vast area of judicially unexamined state and local control. These controls might be motivated by managerial, political, economic, moral, job security, or humanistic goals. The voucher scheme shifts the area for expression of such goals from the total responsibility of a majoritarian board of education to a regulatory scheme which sets some standards and then lets individual schools and parents do as they will.

Opened is the issue of whether we can reestablish this degree of individual and group freedom without simultaneously negating it with a complex of regulations which make everything either required or forbidden. To date, the five states which have passed legislation providing aid to private schools on a purchase-of-services basis,[29] and the two states which have moved toward decentralization of public schools in big cities,[30] have shown little inclination to dis-

27 *Pierce v. Society of Sisters*, 268 U.S. 510 (1925).

28 *See, School District of Abington v. Schempp*, 374 U.S. 203 (1963) in which required Bible readings in public schools were found unconstitutional. The Supreme Court has also invalidated attempts to prohibit foreign language instruction in private schools. *See, Meyer v. Nebraska*, 262 U.S. 390 (1923).

29 Five states have passed purchase-of-services legislation: Michigan, Rhode Island, Ohio, Connecticut, and Pennsylvania. Three of these are presently being contested in the courts. The author modestly refers you to his discussion of the educational impact of these laws appearing in *Saturday Review*, January 16, 1971.

30 Both the Marchi law in New York (Sect. 2590 *et. seq.*) and the Detroit decentralization plan which is presently being litigated have given pitifully little power to local districts. The allocation of powers is in both instances riddled with inconsistencies.

tinguish carefully between necessary minimums and desirable freedoms. Predictably the problem will be the same with any attempt to set up a voucher program—an extreme reluctance to actually expand the range of choice open to parents and schools. The courts may eventually get around to drawing a few distinctions between justifiable and unjustifiable encroachments on individual liberties in education, but the likelihood is that they will generally defer to legislative judgments about such sensitive political matters. For the silver lining one may suppose that the voucher system, because it is ideologically based in individual choice, will cast a greater burden upon the state to justify detailed regulation of the content and method of schooling.

Districting, Transportation, New Schools　Two of the most easily overlooked aspects of voucher schemes involve the inter-related issues of how students are going to get to school and what schools they are going to be able to choose from. It is a problem of defining the range of alternatives, that is, how many schools will be physically accessible and how easy it will be to start new schools to meet unfilled demands.

The transportation problem starts with two questions: Within what geographical area will a parent be able to select a school for his child? Will the voucher be increased in value enough to finance transportation to and from that school? The danger in defining the applicable geographical area is that lines will be drawn which prevent racial or social class integration, much as the town lines of exclusive suburbs do now for the public school system. The most thorough way of insuring that this does not happen would be to constitute the entire state as the set of schools from which a parent may choose. As the area of eligible schools increases, however, so does the transportation bill. Therefore, what is given with one hand—the right to use your voucher at any school in the state—may be taken away with the other—the failure to pay transportation costs for those who need it. It is clear that the full cost of transportation for the poor must be borne by the voucher, or we will simply be using another means to accomplish the same economic segregation which is presently accomplished by neighborhood and suburban boundaries. Every child should get complete transportation costs if he needs it, and no child should receive transportation money if he attends very near his home. There should be no premium placed on staying in the immediate neighborhood.

Recognizing at the outset that people are not going to send their children all over the state for schooling, it is essential that districts in each region of a state be drawn to insure heterogeneity of race, class, and income. Such lines do not force integration; they simply make it possible, and prevent the state from using legal boundaries to thwart the fair admissions policy discussed previously. The formulation of districts within which transportation is provided, and which, therefore, define the range of existing alternatives open to most voucher students, may raise an issue of constitutional magnitude. Either by failing to provide adequate support for transportation, or by districting in a way which *prevents* the establishment of integrated schools, a state might, *de jure*, be thwarting the principles laid down in sixteen years of school segregation cases.

Though it has been little discussed, the districting and transportation issue may be the most sensitive and difficult one to resolve. The problem of drawing districts which are small enough to keep the transportation bill reasonable, but which are mixed racially and socioeconomically, may not be technically difficult. But the willingness to do this will be hard to come by even though the districting enables rather than mandates integration. As with most other attempts at changing the schools, the voucher plan eventually runs headlong into the other areas of American society which must be changed if any part of that interlocking social system is to be made equitable and diverse. Here we are facing the same attitudes which have led to geographical segregation of housing by race. Though free transportation may seem a workable way to overcome this technically, it will not happen without some confrontation on attitudes.

The actual availability of alternatives to the neighborhood school also depends on how easy or difficult it is to start a new school. As anyone who has participated in starting a community or free school can testify, many, if not most, of the problems of getting a learning place going involve the personal energy of the adults and the students. There are, however, a good number of financial, legal, and technical problems which could be alleviated by a well-designed voucher program. The operating costs of the school are already provided by the vouchers, but capital expenditures present a problem of special magnitude to new schools. It would be possible to treat this in two basic ways: either increase the value of the vouchers to cover the amortization of capital expenses, or fund them separately. In either case some guaranteed loan program should be established to insure that a school which otherwise meets the voucher standards does not flounder for inability to get its building or renovations or equipment financed. Something modeled after the Federal Housing Administration and the Federal National Mortgage Association for providing loans when a new school reached a minimum enrollment would probably be suitable.

The legal and technical problems of fitting within the voucher scheme, meeting state standards, and complying with all the applicable state laws could become bothersome to the point of frustration. A voucher design which is serious about encouraging diversity should make comprehensive legal, accounting, and other technical assistance available to any parent, teacher, educator, community organization, or group of students who wish to start a school. Perhaps most important would be the offer of educational assistance to those who are starting new schools. The experiences of the burgeoning community and free schools movement could provide a substantial amount of information on the structuring of new curriculum, new relationships between student, teacher, and parent, and new resources for learning environments.[31]

Technical and educational assistance, like any other resource, can be provided selectively. The voucher system should therefore probably establish several different groups capable of providing such aid to any group starting a new school or seeking to overcome problems with an old one. This perhaps provides the proper role for experts—not control but advice.

Church-State Separation   Comprehending the way in which a voucher scheme would reorganize the provision of public education becomes especially strained when the spectre of a parent choosing a religious school is raised. Though the regulations of the voucher plan aim to maximize a family's ability to choose the education of its preference, when that choice is for religious instruction, a problem of special magnitude develops.

On principle it would seem that respect for diversity ought to include tolerance for religious options, and that there is no more reason to discourage parents from choosing religious schools than military or humanist schools, as long as they all meet minimum state standards and voucher regulations. The First Amendment, however, erects a wall of separation between church and state. Fitting the voucher plan into this context presents a problem which has been overstated.

Historically separation of church and state seems as much as anything to be a response to the need to insulate the political process from religious factionalism, a form of strife which was especially prevalent two hundred years ago and which to some extent is still with us. Religious freedom, like the other individual freedoms protected by the First Amendment, is so much a matter of personal preference and belief that the individual's right to hold these beliefs is deserving of special protection in a society which aims to base itself upon the just consent of the governed. From this point of view any government program or agency which attempts to prescribe individual beliefs or ban group expressions of those beliefs is anathema. Traditionally this analysis has been applied as a justification of separation of church and state. But the amount of socialization and behavior control which characterize the increasingly pervasive public school system raises the question of why we have not been equally concerned with the separation of school and state.

To examine the analogy between the established church, the state, and the

---

31 Models for such assistance are already being set up. In the Bay area in California, SPANNER is a collection of persons and materials available for individuals who need help starting schools or solving problems in existing community schools.

original purposes of the First Amendment on the one hand, and the public school, the state, and the present importance of the First Amendment on the other hand, is a subject for another essay. Some who have thought about this astonishing analogy have come to disconcerting conclusions:

> The difference between the church and the school is mainly that the rites of the school have now become much more rigorous and onerous than the rites of the church in the worst days of the Spanish Inquisition. The school has become the established church of secular times.[32]

That the voucher plan is motivated in part by the desire to disestablish the monolithic school and replace it with a system of diverse and equally available school offerings does not eliminate the constitutional problems which voucher schemes face if they make religious schools eligible. It will be a very long time before the Supreme Court even begins considering the possibility that the aura of personal freedoms protected by the First Amendment ought to prevent an effective public monopoly of schooling. In the meantime, the question remains whether church schools can constitutionally or politically be eligible for voucher students.

Constitutionally it seems plausible that the voucher plan, by channeling money directly to parents and making their choices the operative ones in whether religious or secular schools are aided, avoids violating the First Amendment. There are precedents like the G.I. Bill and Social Security which provide aid to individuals without regulating where they can spend their money and without violating the Constitution. As long as the parent's choice is unencumbered, that is, as long as the voucher system remains neutral with regard to which religious school or whether any religious school is chosen, it is at least arguable that the voucher scheme rests squarely on the voluntarism which the First Amendment protects.[33]

Fortunately, there is not room here for a discussion of the legal intricacies which would put a voucher scheme within the purview of the First Amendment. One has the feeling that the emotional energy has gone out of this particular debate, or that when it is there, it is misplaced. Efforts to provide state aid to nonpublic schools, coming largely from Catholic quarters,[34] have been directed largely at purchase-of-services arrangements. There is a good deal of political muscle behind these proposals; and it is sad that the efforts serve almost none of the goals of diversity, racial equality, equal resource distribution,

32 Ivan Illich, "Commencement at the University of Puerto Rico," *New York Review of Books*, Vol. 13, October 9, 1969.

33 For a discussion of voluntarism, *see*, Judith Areen, "Public Aid to Non-Public Schools: A Breach in the Sacred Wall?" in a future issue of the *Case Institute Law Review*.

34 It is reported that the 1970 census shows that there are about 50 million Catholics in the United States.

and voluntarism which a voucher scheme could plausibly advance. The political issue is not so much whether religious schools will be aided by the states, but whether the form of that aid will be conducive to needed reforms of public education or will simply reinforce the only two options most families have at present—the established public monolith or the Catholic school system.

Breaking the Consumer Analogy In each of the problem areas specified—economic model, admissions policies, accountability, the range of alternatives, and separation of church and state—it seems rationally possible that a system could be designed which meets the need for racial equality, redistribution of wealth, respect for genuine value diversity and the objective conditions for improvement in schooling. A great deal of experimenting will be needed to find out whether these projections are in fact realizable. But today's political complexion discourages belief that the will to achieve these goals really exists. Reasonable experimentation, therefore, may not get a fair chance.

But even if this rational scheme could be converted into a political reality, one is still left with an almost metaphorical mistrust of the idea. This mistrust seems to grow out of the analogy which has so often been drawn between a voucher scheme and a regulated market system. If you have tried to buy an automobile which does not pollute the air, or have had any of the myriad other experiences in which it is demonstrated that decisions which are economically advantageous to profit-making corporations are usually disadvantageous to the public interest, this analogy is probably very disturbing. If you are poor and have suffered the degradation and deprivation which others usually brush off as an unfortunate side effect of the system which keeps the country great, the analogy may become a compelling reason to oppose vouchers.

Those who have described the system as one which is based upon the benefits of introducing economic competition into schooling certainly have raised this spectre by their failure to suggest a means of avoiding the hazards of a consumer system. The fears generated in this situation seem to be based on three aspects of consumer systems—the separation of consumer from producer, the presence of the profit motive, and the use of advertising or hucksterism. Some modifications in the voucher idea could be suggested to break the connection between free choice and these three worrisome characteristics.

In the present scheme of public schooling, formal accountability rests largely upon voter choices made in electing school boards, while informal accountability is a response to pressure groups. The voucher scheme seeks to couple with this individual parental control over a per capita share of finances for schooling. As significant an addition to parental power as this may be, however, it would probably constitute a net loss over the present system if it became a substitute for more direct political control. Imagine a school system composed of a diverse collection of schools run by public authorities, private business corporations, teachers' collectives, parent groups, and community development corporations. The only parental power (other than voting for those who set state minimum standards) would rest on consumer choice from among whatever options the schooling "producers" happen to be offering. One can, of course, start his own school, and there is assistance available for doing this, but essentially the choice is limited in the same way as it presently is in most consumer markets. The means of production is not controlled by the people who must make do with what is produced, and so it is possible for producers to manipulate and restrict their offerings for their own purposes. Under such conditions it is probably wishful thinking to say that parents will have more power over the nature of schooling or that the schools will need to be more responsive.

One possible remedy for this would be to create for all voucher schools a required corporate form which would have the effect of putting the parents of the school's students in control of their school. This might be accomplished by making the parents of every entering child a voting member of the school's governing board, with the provision that the parent relinquish his franchise when his child graduated from the school. The powers of the governing board would have to be spelled out carefully to insure that parents did, in fact, have substantial and important authority, while protecting the ability of the school's director to function effectively. The governing board would then be the "local school board" for the particular school involved, and the locus of discretion over school policy would simply have been shifted from a city-wide to a single school board. Adopting such a required form for voucher schools would mean that rather than substituting consumer power for electoral power over school policy, the two would become additive on the decentralized scale of individual schools. The voucher scheme would then have not only an admissions regulation which minimized discrimination, but a governance form which provided community control. Those parents who did not wish to participate in policy-making could simply not participate, and those who did want to would be able to avoid endless controversy over their right to do so. The spectre of the helpless or ignorant consumer would at least be reduced to a problem of the same magnitude as the helpless or ignorant voter, while paternalism might be kept to a minimum.

The analogy with the consumer market might be further attenuated by prohibiting profit-making companies (and their non-profit subsidiaries or affiliates) from running voucher schools. While profit may no longer be the center of corporate motives,[35] there is really no reason to use the profit motive in the

35 A. A. Berle discusses what may have replaced the profit motive for large corporations in *Twentieth Century Capitalism*. New York: Harcourt, Brace, 1954.

provision of schooling. Too much has been made of the idea that economic competition in schooling will increase its quality. More likely, economic competition will increase efficiency at the expense of quality, much as it does elsewhere, through adoption of a restricted and materialistic set of goals. Moreover, the kinds of capital and corporate image advertising advantages which business corporations would have in running schools would soon allow them to dominate the field, thereby giving antihumanist, managerial goals even greater hegemony over schooling.

It is possible, of course, that businesses might run the best vocational or technical schools. The trouble with their participation is not this, but that they tend to assume that training for existing or projected jobs is all there is to education. The result is schools which become, even more than they are now, service organizations for the technological society. Service to the corporate structure becomes more important than questioning the values on which the structure is based. Students become so many potential cogs in the machine, needing only a little shaping here and honing there. At the end of the conveyor belt, of course, there are better jobs for better pay to be better consumers of what the corporations make.

Given the amount of socialization which takes place in a school, whatever its limited technical or vocational aims, it makes little sense to put schooling in the hands of those whose self-interest is largely the preservation of the status quo and the most extensive control of "resources" and "markets" possible. These "factory metaphors," as Thomas Green has called them, portend a system of education "in which schools are assessed primarily by the utility of their 'product' to other institutions of society—most notably its economic and military institutions."[36] Education is a personal and community process, and anything which makes it likely that a national or international technocracy will replace personal initiative and direction in education is unacceptable.

The third method of breaking the consumer-voucher analogy would involve restrictions on advertising. It has already been indicated that schools would be required to provide parents with certain basic information, so that informed choice would be possible. To this might be added an absolute dollar limit on advertising expenses, much in the way that we might beneficially reduce political hucksterism by limiting television campaign spending in national elections.

Children's Rights or Parents' Rights   A second major unexamined problem in most voucher schemes concerns the comparative interests of parents and children. It is always assumed that the family will receive the voucher and that the family will make the choice of schools. A look

---

36   Thomas Green, *op. cit.*

at some of the controversies over schooling indicates, however, that there is often quite a gap between what the parents think is a good education and what the students think. There is, in addition, the very real question of whether a child reaching the age of thirteen or fourteen shouldn't have the right to determine much more about his present and future than the usual chattel theory of children allows. All of this may be a problem of educating parents about their children and vice versa—indeed, bringing parents into closer contact with the problems of schooling and children is one benefit a voucher scheme might produce—but the basic structural problem of how much influence young people will retain over schooling remains. To some, the issue is merely whether students should be protected from themselves by their parents or the state.

One suggestion for securing further influence for students has been to give them the vouchers after age thirteen. Since they still remain economically dependent on their parents in other respects, however, it is unclear how this plan would help them without causing excessive strife within the family. Another possibility would be to give students over a certain age voting power within voucher schools through requirements in the corporate form. The disadvantage of this idea is that it does not deal with the initial choice of schools. This question plays upon so many values which require rethinking and refeeling that it is undoubtedly safest to bring the discussion of it to an abrupt end with the statement that it requires more thought.

Voucher Politics   At this point the structural nature of voucher schemes and most of the ways of manipulating the variables have been outlined. If each variable in the structure were arranged ideally, what might result? Public and private education would essentially be redefined. The uniting of the best aspects of each would be a set of independent schools, all of which would be free[37] (in the sense of being paid for out of tax dollars); schools would be equally accessible to all; and control of quality would be divided between minimum standards set by the state and policy decisions reached or approved by parents or students in each independent school.

---

37 If the Coons plan of family power equalizing were adopted, each family would pay a small self-tax, and education would not be "free" in the sense of separating the payment of taxes from the granting of benefits. Since these payments are calculated on the basis of a progressive tax schedule, however, all but the psychological impact of the payment is exactly as it would be in a traditionally "free" school tax system. The self-tax serves as a measure of the importance of education to the family. Arguments that the self-tax percentage also corresponded to the private benefit of education to the family have been made. But it would appear that these are more soundly grounded in theoretical economics than in education theory. *See,* for example, John Dewey. *Democracy and Education.* New York: Macmillan, 1916, which makes it plain that education is personal in totality.

Further, this decentralized system would allow maximum choice to families by providing them with the means to choose any school within a wide geographical area, and by insuring that any alternative would receive state support if it could attract families which valued its services. The notion that for the poor and middle class there is only one definition of good education, that arrived at by the public school monopoly, would be abandoned.

Under such a system the advantages we might hope for would be these:

—Halting the present situation in which only the rich and those with support from religious institutions can escape public schools, and in which economic and class separation is made easy.

—Shifting the source of initiative for school reform to families by making it possible for them to exercise more choice.

—Increasing economic and political power of individuals over their children's education.

—Making possible not only geographically decentralized schools, but school communities based on many other shared values.

—Providing effective means for preventing racial and economic discrimination and for insuring the presence of adequate resources for all school children.

—Increasing the diversity of American education and its ability to experiment by encouraging alternative schools and breaking down the present public school monopoly.

—Reducing the size of decision-making units and encouraging a less bureaucratic relationship between school and family.

—Removing the state from determination of educational policy except as regards absolute minimums (preventing discrimination, insuring equal resources, providing basic information, securing minimum educational standards).

—Supporting the growing movement of community schools and free schools.

Since the voucher scheme is so malleable in its basic design, it is also possible that the result of adopting it, if it were fashioned by the wrong political motives, would be to aggravate each of the problems to which the preceding list refers. The introduction to the OEO feasibility study notes that "... an unregulated voucher scheme could be the most serious setback for the education of disadvantaged children in the history of the United States." In this context arguing that vouchers are either good or bad is the same as describing the kind of voucher scheme one advocates.

The basic difficulty with the voucher idea is that it requires a political commitment to values which are very weak and vulnerable in America today: a commitment to equality of wealth, power, and race; respect for and encouragement of real pluralism; nonintervention by government in substantial educational decisions; high regard for individuals and children; encouraging social integration; placing personalism and communitarianism above bureaucracy and technocratic values. It is hard to see where the support for a good voucher system will come from. It is likely that were a voucher scheme adopted by the states tomorrow, it would reflect the same values which are presently aggravating the abominable situation of American education.

This, of course, is not the way it should be. The present situation in schooling and in the country generally is one in which we desperately need to let values and institutions develop from the people up. Continued top down efforts to cope with dissatisfaction by tightening the controls of existing institutions or making a few fine adjustments in the machine cannot be responsive to the basic changes in consciousness which are taking place. We need to give ourselves more space. We need to open up and in some cases even terminate institutions voluntarily. The voucher plan can be drawn so that it provides this needed space for development of new learning relationships, while at the same time guarding against the basic discriminations which we have been suffering.

The political distance between where we are and where we would like to be is great. The base of support for a decent voucher system is quite small at present both because a voucher scheme is abstract, and because it is unclear whether, as a slogan, education vouchers are the property of conservative or radical forces. The greatest need at present is not to decide whether vouchers are good or bad—that is entirely premature and overly academic—but to organize a base of support which has it in its self-interest and political ideology to press for the values upon which a good voucher scheme would be based. Such an organizing strategy can be based on pointing out the inadequacies of the present school system, demonstrating that these problems often stem from the political structure of schooling, and supporting efforts to decentralize and diversify power and increase resources. At the same time, a complete strategy would support the community and free school movement, for this movement is not only the most dependable political base for a fair voucher system, it is a manifestation of some of the schools which might arise under such a system.

In fact, free schools and community schools provide the most convincing evidence of the benefits of a voucher plan. Arguments about decentralized decision-making, equal resource allocation, personalism, and pluralism are persuasive; but they remain arguments. The existence of an organic and growing movement which is starting independent, experimental schools and serving minority groups goes beyond argument. It is evidence of what people are actually doing with their desire for useful education and free learning. It is evidence that a voucher plan would be supporting something which exists, instead of creating a system out of abstractions in the heads of social planners. It is evidence that things which are now struggling to happen in spite of the presence of public institutions could be freely happening with the aid of public institutions.

Voucher schemes require us to take a comprehensive look at the political and structural aspects of schooling, and to get to the basic value questions which we generally ignore or cannot bear to face. Perhaps this is why the idea is supported so much by slogans or dismissed so easily by flippancy. In any case, it will not be really clear whether or not the idea is beneficial until enough political forces have lined up to see who is in a position to fashion its design. In the meantime, vouchers may be considered a revolutionary idea, for like other revolutions, it does not matter so much who starts it as who gains control of it once it has begun.

The Economics of the Voucher System

Eli Ginzberg is A. Barton Hepburn Professor
of Economics and director of the Conservation
of Human Resources Project at Columbia
University. In this paper, Professor Ginzberg
criticizes the economic assumptions underlying
the voucher proposal.

Eli Ginzberg, "The Economics of the Voucher System," Teachers College Record, *Vol. 72,
No. 3 (February 1971), pp. 373-382.*

Eli Ginzberg

One of the first proponents of the voucher system for education in the United States was Milton Friedman of the University of Chicago, who argued that its adoption would lead to a series of improvements: individual (parental) freedom through broadened consumer choice; efficiency and economy by introducing competition where monopoly had earlier held sway; and diversity through an increase in entrepreneurship. Friedman knew that in sparsely settled areas conditions of scale might inhibit the introduction of multiple schools, and he recognized that among population groups committed to the maintenance of segregation the voucher system would be welcomed. But Friedman argued for "freedom," even if it would force Negroes to wait for a changed attitude among whites before they could attend desegregated schools.

The Cambridge group which recently developed the planning document for the Office of Economic Opportunity explored whether the voucher system might be used to speed certain specific educational objectives: increased diversity in curricula and teaching methods; desegregation; increased opportunities for minority children to attend better schools; greater parental choice; more disclosure of information from schools competing for any type of public support; and the use of public funds for the financially vulnerable parochial school system.

The Cambridge group is principally concerned with better education for children from low income families and minority groups. It is fair to say that, if this "redistributive" effort cannot be accomplished, these proponents of the voucher system will not be interested in an experiment to test its other potentialities.

Lessons from a Pluralistic Economy   Our society has attempted for several decades to establish better conditions for the poor and otherwise disadvantaged on a series of fronts, namely, housing, welfare, income, health, as well as education. The results of these experiences deserve attention, even if, in so doing, we must ignore certain refinements.

After twenty-five years of effort, we must realize that even with substantial public funds available to force the issue, the progress made in improving housing available to the poor, particularly on an integrated basis, has been slow. While there are a few partially successful experiments, even in such a "liberal" community as New York City whites are still willing to forego more and better space and lower rents in order not to live in projects and neighborhoods with large numbers of blacks.

With regard to welfare, the 91st Congress refused to pass the Administration's Family Assistance Plan, which would make the federal government responsible for establishing and underwriting a welfare floor of $1,600 per family throughout the United States. Congress is hesitant to accept a responsibility previously covered by state and local governments, especially when the starting cost looms high, that is, over $4 billion annually.

On the income front we have done little with regard to redistribution. Since the end of World War II, the proportion of total disposable income available to families with incomes in the lowest quintile has not increased. Belatedly (1969), Congress eliminated the federal income tax liability for families at the lower end of the scale, but this will not have more than a marginal effect on their net position.

The record of the expansion and improvement of health services for the poor shows that Medicare is paying about 45 percent of the total costs of medical care for the aged, while Medicare premiums have to be repeatedly raised to stay abreast of the rapidly accelerating costs. Despite the expenditure of several billions of dollars annually, it is hard to prove that the quantity and quality of medical services available to the poor have been significantly increased under Medicaid. This much is sure: Both the federal and state governments are unable to keep pouring more money into Medicaid. Since the health care system for the poor remains seriously deficient, the country is beginning to talk about the need for national health insurance in the belief that it might accomplish for all what Medicaid was expected but was unable to do for some.

On the basis of this summary review, the following deductions can be ventured about governmental engendered efforts to bring about substantial improvements in the quantity and quality of services available to the poor and disadvantaged:

a) The programs involve expenditures of many billions of dollars annually.

b) The expectations on which they are based are seldom, if ever, fulfilled.

c) Congress is hesitant to assume large financial commitments previously carried by state and local governments.

d) The expenditure of increased sums does not insure the delivery of more and better services to a targeted population such as the poor.

e) Many white families, in the North as well as in the South, will forego the advantages provided by governmental subsidies if they can be enjoyed only by close association with blacks.

It is irresponsible to move ahead with even an experimental program of educational vouchers without facing up to the results of these recent efforts at distributive justice. The American people have already expended to little avail many tens of billions of dollars in recent years to achieve objectives closely related to those subsumed under this latest version of educational reform.

Recent Educational Reforms Reappraised We will now take a closer look at the efforts that have been launched and implemented in recent years to achieve the goal which is the essence of the proposed educational vouchers, the goal of improving the schooling available to low income and minority youngsters.

In quick review, we note first the introduction of governmental financing for preschool programs. Head Start made it possible for the children of many black and other poor families to attend nursery schools which formerly had catered to parents who were able and willing to pay. But with minor exceptions, this departure provided a service that saw little commingling of children from different backgrounds. Head Start programs have been overwhelmingly directed to establishing new institutions to serve the disadvantaged. It is questionable whether any significant expansion would have taken place had government stipulated that the poor and the black be admitted in large numbers to existing, predominantly white, middle-class nursery schools.

A second major thrust has been the effort led by the federal government, reinforced by state and local governments, to make supplemental resources available to schools which are attended overwhelmingly by children from disadvantaged homes. Two findings come clear: despite the legislative interest, much of the additional money ended up in programs available to children from middle and even upper income homes. Similarly, advisors to the Department of Health, Education, and Welfare have been able to determine that the improvement grants resulted in no appreciable gain in the educational achievement of the children who were the target of the effort.

Under the combination of legislative, judicial, and administrative pressure, reinforced in certain areas by political pressure and public opinion, some progress has been made to broaden the opportunities for black youngsters to attend schools previously not open to them where the student body has been exclusively or predominantly white and where the level of student achievement has been considerably higher than in all-black schools.

For a variety of reasons, including cost or length of transportation, student and teacher hostility, fear, preference for remaining with one's own group, many black families able to enroll their children for the first time in predominantly white schools did not avail themselves of this option.

In many communities the black leadership has recently become more interested in securing control over ghetto schools in the belief that they have more to gain thereby than in pursuing the goal of desegregation which is often logistically impossible and which in any case would fail many black children by stressing white, middle-class values. These leaders are saying to their local boards of education: give us the tools and we will do the job of educating our youngsters.

Finally, in harmony with the temper of the times, many parochial and private schools which were formerly closed to blacks or which admitted only a select few have changed their admission policies to admit many more, both paying and scholarship students.

Let us distill the principal findings from two decades of educational reform:

a) It proved easier for the federal government to start a separate preschool program for disadvantaged children than to have them admitted into the existing institutions which were in no position to cope with large numbers of new youngsters.

b) It proved easier for government to provide several billion dollars of additional educational funding annually than to see that the money accrued to the advantage of the targeted disadvantaged population.

c) The black community has become increasingly uneasy about the practicality or desirability of school desegregation, and accordingly, in many localities it has opted for control over ghetto schools.

d) The proportion of black students in parochial and private schools on a paying or scholarship basis has increased substantially in recent years.

A Close Look at Educational Vouchers   We are now in a better position to look more closely at the proposal for instituting a system of educational vouchers and to appraise the prospects that the planners' priority objectives will be achieved. We will leave until the concluding section our assessment of the desirability of such a plan, even if it proved to be feasible.

The Cambridge group's proposal has the following components:

a) The voucher system would cover the full operating cost of education, thereby encouraging the expansion of a diversity of nonpublic schools.

b) The vouchers for disadvantaged children would be worth more than those for middle- and upper-income families, which would facilitate the admission of the disadvantaged to preferred private schools.

c) Discrimination would be controlled by administrative surveillance; the participating private schools would be compelled to admit at least half their student body by lottery.

d) Vouchers would be given directly to parents who, having received information from the educational authorities about competing schools, could make an effective choice.

Let us look at what is implied in realizing these desiderata.

Re (a): A full-cost voucher system.

1. The proposal carries with it a certain increase in governmental operating expenditures for public education of approximately 10 to 15 percent, or about $5 billion annually for elementary and secondary education alone.

2. A full-cost voucher system would lead to the maintenance of the present parochial schools and their proliferation. Since most blacks are Protestants and most parochial schools are Catholic or Jewish, it is difficult to see how this trend could be advantageous to blacks.

3. The objective of assuring more blacks and other disadvantaged children access to good private schools hinges on the establishment of new schools and their ability to provide better education at the average cost per pupil in the public school.

4. Under a voucher system, the subsequent withdrawal of sizeable numbers of white and black pupils from existing public schools would raise the existing per capita cost. The advocates of the voucher system might respond that even if the average cost were increased it would be accompanied by an improvement in quality. In any case, we must anticipate more need for the taxpayer to increase his support of education.

5. The voucher system, per se, would not contribute to narrowing the striking differentials in per capita expenditures that currently exist among states and among localities within the same state.

Re (b): The vouchers of disadvantaged children would be worth more, thereby facilitating their acceptance at private schools.

1. The Cambridge group indicates that it believes the special financing that would be necessary could come only from the federal government. Whether it would be forthcoming is, to put it conservatively, moot.

2. The assumption that there is an easy way to determine which families would be entitled to a more valuable voucher is an assumption contrary to fact, given the variability in both income and expenditures over short periods. Moreover, as the Cambridge group itself recognizes, the fact that a student is black or poor does not imply that he will be more difficult to educate. In that event why should the community provide the school with an override in tuition?

3. If the proposal were acceptable to the taxpayers, it might go a small distance toward facilitating the admission of disadvantaged children to desirable private schools, but only the number and proportion that these schools would be willing to admit, subject to the pressures that might be exercised on them as noted below.

Re (c): Discrimination would be controlled by administrative surveillance and by a lottery for admission.

1. We noted earlier that the majority of private schools at the present time are under religious auspices. It is highly improbable that any level of government would seek to force such institutions to accept large numbers of black and other disadvantaged children unless they were of the same faith, or that minority groups would press in large numbers to be admitted.

2. The better nondenominational private schools currently spend 50 to 150 percent more per pupil than the public school. Yet under the plan proposed by the Cambridge group, no voucher school would be permitted to charge additional tuition. The import of such a regulation should be clear. If affluent parents are willing to invest several thousand dollars annually in the education of their children, these high tuition schools would not participate in the voucher plan. One possible consequence would be a *reduction* in the number of minority children whom these schools accept once other alternatives become available.

3. This brings us face-to-face with the challenge of discrimination. In communities where the number of minority children seeking admission to a private school is small, the predominantly white schools might be willing to accept 50 percent of all admissions on a lottery basis on the assumption that the number of minority youngsters they would be forced to admit would fall between 10 to 20 percent. But it is questionable whether most schools would participate if the distribution between white and black might end up closer to fifty-fifty.

Re (d): Vouchers would be given to parents who, provided with information by the educational authorities, could make an effective choice among schools.

1. The Cambridge group acknowledges that it is difficult and at present impossible to provide definitive information about the performance of a school because of disagreement about the goals of education, the need to balance short and long run outcomes, the inability to distinguish what the child brings into class from what the school does for him, the absence of reliable measuring instruments, and further difficulties.

2. In a period such as the present, one must consider the influence of demagogic leadership in persuading ghetto parents to opt for one or another alternative. We do not postulate, as the proponents of the voucher system appear to do, that each parent will make a decision on his own.

3. The question of relevant information is more complicated if we assume that many new private schools will spring up as a result of the introduction of a voucher system. Before several years have passed, how can we

know anything about the performance of the new schools, even if the criteria are limited to what the children report?

4. On the basis of recent experience which has involved the participation of parents in the education of their children, it is venturesome to postulate that many ghetto parents will have the time, energy, interest, and background necessary to make informed judgments, even if the available information were much better than now appears likely. Yet this is a critical dimension of the voucher plan.

Some Economic Speculations The voucher plan, at least as prepared by the Cambridge group, aims to improve the schooling opportunities available to the black and the poor by increasing their prospects for entering good private schools and simultaneously encouraging the creation of new schools outside the present bureaucratic structure. As far as the first objective is concerned, we have seen that it is predicated on the taxpayers' not only making more money available for education in general, but agreeing to spend an extra sum for the education of the disadvantaged. Even if we grant that these two assumptions are realistic, we noted that more is required. The existing private schools would have to adjust their admission policies and procedures to accept a larger number of disadvantaged children. While some would, the question remains how many would enter the system. We argued that the number would be small given the following facts: most private schools are under denominational auspices, and the better nondenominational schools are unlikely to cooperate if their proportion of black and poor children exceeds 20 percent or so. Hence the voucher plan must be assessed specifically from the viewpoint of its contribution to the establishment of new schools that would be superior to those currently in existence.

Economists have long proceeded on the assumption that entrepreneurship is a scarce resource. To assume that there are many people capable of bringing new schools into existence, staffing them, and structuring curricula that would be more attuned to the needs and interests of the student body is a presumption contrary to fact. If the existing private schools are unlikely to accept many disadvantaged youngsters under the voucher plan, and if well-run schools will be difficult to bring into existence, there is little basis for following the voucher route.

There are several additional dimensions to the establishment of new schools. The Cambridge group is as silent on the matter of funds for new construction as it is on the purchase of units that are currently part of the governmental system. It is unlikely that hard-pressed taxpayers will view with favor additional funds for new construction on the ground that "competition" will have beneficial effects on performance. Moreover, if educational costs are not to be increased unnecessarily, an area planning mechanism would have to assess the need for additional capacity and to choose among competing sponsors, public or private, with the decision almost certainly going in favor of the public sector.

A possible alternative would be the sale of existing public schools to private sponsors. Milton Friedman contemplated this in his original proposal. But the odds are strongly against such sales, among other reasons because of lack of requisite capital by the new sponsors. Moreover, one must allow for strong resistance toward the dismemberment of the public system by the educational leadership as well as by suspicious taxpayers.

A related matter that bears on this issue of a potential shift in ownership involves the long-range contractual commitments held by the teaching and administrative staffs covering tenure, increments based on years of service, pension rights, and related employment benefits. The troubles of 1968 in Ocean Hill-Brownsville should serve as a warning that, even if school buildings could be sold or transferred to a new management, the legal commitments to staff represent a barrier that makes such transfers exceedingly difficult.

The basic premise underlying the voucher system is the belief in the benefits of increased competition. But economists have long recognized that effective competition presupposes some approximation to equality of bargaining power. And that is missing in the case of the poor and the disadvantaged. By virtue of more income, more political power, and housing discrimination, middle-class whites have succeeded in removing themselves from close contact with disadvantaged blacks. It is fatuous to believe that the white community will permit a voucher system to operate so as to remove the barriers that they have laboriously erected to protect themselves and their children from what they consider to be the undesirable behavior patterns of the disadvantaged.

The other nub of the voucher proposal is to make more funds available to improve the quality of educational services available to disadvantaged children in the ghetto, preferably outside the present rigid educational system. But as we noted previously, the presumption against such an effort's succeeding is powerful given the shortages of entrepreneurial talent, lack of command over facilities, and long-term personnel arrangements governing the present staff.

Gimmick versus Institutional Reform The voucher system is a gimmick. It pretends to offer a solution to segregated schools and ineffective education for the poor and disadvantaged. Let us remember that it has taken sixteen years of judicial, legislative, and administrative pressure on the part of the federal government to make some headway in desegregating public schools in the South. While much remains to be accomplished, the last several years have seen progress. In the North, the situation has worsened as a result of demographic changes and housing patterns. More and more black children attend schools where most of the student body is black. The incontestable fact is that significant desegregation of the public school hinges on the prior re-distribution of the urban minority population which would reduce its high concentration. Without housing desegregation, not much progress can be expected on the educational front—surely not in the elementary grades.

During the past decade various levels of government have sought to increase their educational expenditures for disadvantaged pupils in the hope and expectation of improving their experiences and adding to their skills. The results to date have been unimpressive. There is nothing new in the voucher plan that addresses this problem of improving the performance of ghetto schools through larger expenditures per capita, other than to facilitate the establishment or expansion of schools outside the public system. But for reasons that have been adduced above, the outlook for new sponsorship is not propitious. Moreover, the question remains open whether new sponsorship would lead to improved educational fare and results for the disadvantaged child.

Desegregation and improved education for black and other poor children are not social objectives that can be easily accomplished in a society that remains heavily racist, unbalanced in its population distributions, and that has no effective way of relating additional educational inputs to educational achievement. It is a presumption based on faith, not facts, that a gadget such as a system of educational vouchers will succeed in resolving a problem in which the Supreme Court, Congress, state and local legislatures have had but modest success, despite resort to police power and the expenditure of many billions of dollars.

A Trial Balance Sheet   Recourse to a voucher system, even under the safeguards recommended by the Cambridge group which will not necessarily be adopted or enforced by many jurisdictions, promises to accomplish the following:

a) To shore up parochial schools.
b) To encourage black nationalists in the ghetto to start up and operate their own schools.
c) To ease the tax burden on upper-middle-class families who now send their children to private schools.
d) To increase the number of mediocre private schools.
e) To weaken an already weak public educational system in cities with a high proportion of minority population.
f) To facilitate the increase of small numbers of black and poor students at parochial and private schools.
g) To weaken the forces operating to enforce desegregation in public schools.

There are good reasons for citizens to be concerned about the halting progress which we have made to speed school desegregation and to improve the quality of education for the ghetto child. The effective reform of the large city school systems will not be easy, which helps to explain why a White House Task Force some years ago, in an unpublished report, unanimously recommended the establishment in each major metropolis of a competitive system of education subsidized by large federal funds for a period of a decade or more. Here was a remedy cut to size. The voucher system is not. Moreover, vouchers threaten many values that need reinforcing, not weakening. The country needs institutional reforms, not more gimmicks.

Vouchers and the Citizen — Some Legal Questions

Walter McCann is chairman of the program
in educational administration and associate
professor of education at Harvard University.
Judith Areen, at the Center for the Study
of Public Policy, Cambridge, was a member
of the team that prepared the feasibility study
on vouchers for the Office of Economic
Opportunity. In this essay, the authors provide
the legal rationale for the CSPP regulated
voucher.

Walter McCann and Judith Areen, "Vouchers and the Citizen—Some Legal Questions,"
Teachers College Record, *Vol. 72, No. 3 (February 1971), pp. 389-404.*

Walter McCann
Judith Areen

Displaying unusual humility for a member of the legal profession, Mr. Justice Jackson once warned the Supreme Court that it must avoid becoming the "super board of education for every school district in the nation."[1] Thoughtful lawyers and judges are justifiably reluctant to intervene in school matters, but they are continually called upon to deal with legal matters which inevitably influence the education of children. Probably no single event has had more impact on the shape of American education in the last fifteen years than the Supreme Court's decision in *Brown v. The Board of Education*.[2] There is little evidence that courts and lawyers, or professors for that matter, are overwhelmingly qualified to make educational policy. Yet they will continue to wind up in that position as long as educators, students, and parents ask, as they must, "what the law is" on particular issues.

This discussion of the "law" on education vouchers should be read, therefore, with some skepticism. The ability of lawyers to predict what the courts might do with such a radically new approach to public education is unavoidably limited. More importantly, educators must be wary lest important educational decisions needlessly become the captive of tentative legal predictions. Sound educational planning should ultimately control the shape of educational change, whether it be voucher plans or something else, not quick acquiescence to supposed legal barriers which might be removed by appropriate legislation.

Here we will focus on three of the legal issues most often raised in discussion of voucher systems: race, religion, and maintaining quality in schools. State constitutions and laws vary widely in their treatment of these issues, particularly of religion. Because exhaustive treatment is beyond the scope of this article, and probably the patience of its readers, most of the discussion, therefore, will focus on federal standards and cases, although representative state laws will be discussed where appropriate.

1 *Illinois ex rel. McCollum v. Board of Education*, 333 U.S. 203, 237 (1948) (concurring opinion).
2 *Brown v. Board of Education*, 347 U.S. 483 (1954).

Complicating the analysis are the many quite different programs which huddle under the rubric education vouchers. Furthermore, legal questions cannot easily be answered in the abstract. Is aid to religious schools constitutional? Are voucher systems legally permissible? Is racial balance required? Ask a lawyer these questions and the unsatisfying response is predictable: "It depends." It depends on the particular facts, plans, and programs under scrutiny. It depends on how things would work. We will try to reduce the tangle of dependency in our legal analysis by dealing generally with the regulated model proposed by the Center for the Study of Public Policy to the Office of Economic Opportunity, both because we are most familiar with that plan and because it embodies the education safeguards most consistent with the Constitution. We begin, then, with a brief outline of the proposed voucher plan.

Brief Description   The Center has proposed that vouchers or tuition grants be made available on a demonstration basis to parents of elementary school children. The vouchers would be roughly equal to the present per pupil expenditure level in the public schools, with suitable adjustments for rental and renovation costs over the duration of the experiment. Parents could use a voucher to pay the education costs of their child at the school of their choice as long as the school agreed to three conditions: 1. to charge parents no tuition in excess of the voucher level; 2. to admit students without regard to race and to allocate at least one half of the open places randomly among the applicants to the school (as long as there were fewer applicants than places, random allocation would be unnecessary); and 3. to provide to parents all information about the school requested by the local group running the voucher demonstration. In addition, the Center has recommended that compensatory funds be provided to supplement the vouchers of educationally disadvantaged students. This would provide funds for the additional costs of their education and an incentive to schools to admit these students.[3]

Many existing private schools presently charge tuition far in excess of the public school expenditures. They would undoubtedly find the limitation unacceptable. Under the proposed voucher system, they would probably continue to operate as they do now, without public funds. But a new market would be created. Some schools would undoubtedly believe that they could offer strong educational opportunities for the same cost as public schools, and with the required open admissions policy. The tuition limit might seem to dampen the possibilities for increasing the amount of resources available to schools, but it need not. First, schools are free to raise funds from sources other than tuition.

---

3 For a more complete discussion of the plan, *see, Education Vouchers: A Report on Financing Education by Grants to Parents.* Prepared by the Center for the Study of Public Policy, Cambridge, Massachusetts, December, 1970.

Second, more families would have a stake in increasing public school funds (families with students now in parochial schools, for example). They would perhaps be less likely to oppose needed tax increases. Most important, the tuition limitation prevents public subvention of economically exclusive schools. Public funding of such schools could well usher in a system of education even more segregated by family income, not to mention race or class, than the present sorry situation.

The admissions restrictions also aim to preserve equality of access to voucher schools. Other approaches, quotas for one, might protect against invidious racial discrimination. Yet other, more subtle, forms of grouping could lead to the same undesirable results. Random admissions to at least half the places in an oversubscribed school protects against other less easily identified, yet equally destructive, practices, such as discrimination against slow learners. Note that the proposed random admissions requirement applies only to *applicants*.

Finally, the information requirement is critical. Parents must be well informed about available schools and their differences. Creation of more diverse school opportunities would otherwise serve little purpose. With that information, plus the economic power to choose among schools, the assumption is that parents will make wise decisions for their children. This assumption is not universally shared, but it is at least as believable as the assumption that inflexible geographic zoning is a wise and equitable way to dole out educational opportunities.

Vouchers and Racial Discrimination   Voucher critics have expressed genuine concern that financing education by payments to parents would lead to racial segregation in the schools. This charge must be faced squarely, even though it is disingenuous not to balance it against the reality of our already highly segregated schools. While some voucher systems (such as the Friedman unregulated model) might well lead to more racial segregation, a happy coincidence of education and legal policy appears to prevail in this area. Such systems seem as constitutionally suspect as they are educationally undesirable.

Six Southern states, at one time or another, have attempted to establish "tuition voucher programs." They were designed to avoid dismantling segregated "dual" public school systems by channeling public funds to segregated private schools. The more significant historical fact, however, is that all six efforts were held unconstitutional by the courts; there is every reason to predict the same fate for any similar attempts, either in the North or the South.[4]

4 *See, Coffey v. State Educational Finance Commission*, 296 F. Supp. 1389 (S.D. Miss. 1969); *Griffin v. State Board of Education*, 296 F. Supp. 1178 (E.D. Va. 1969); *Brown v. South Carolina State Board of Education*, 296 F. Supp. 199 (D.S. Car. 1968), *aff'd per*

First, past case decisions firmly hold that government may not avoid providing citizens with the equal protection of the laws by conducting essentially public functions behind an artificial veil of "private" sponsorship. Under this policy (known as the "state action doctrine") various "private" organizations have been held subject to the constitutional obligations usually imposed on the state by the equal protection clause of the Fourteenth Amendment: a political party which prevented blacks from voting in the party primary;[5] a restaurant located in a state building;[6] a community park;[7] and a hospital which received federal and state subsidies.[8] While few private schools have so far been held subject to the equal protection clause,[9] a "private" school which received public funds via vouchers would seem inexorably subject to that provision of the Fourteenth Amendment.

Once subject to the state action doctrine, a private school would be treated essentially like any public school with regard to racial discrimination. This leaves unresolved the difficult issues of legal differences between "accidental" (de facto) segregation and governmentally fostered (de jure) segregation.[10]

---

curiam, 393 U.S. 222; Poindexter v. Louisiana Financial Assistance Commission, 275 F. Supp. 833 (E.D. La. 1967), aff'd per curiam, 389 U.S. 571 (1968); Lee v. Macon County Board of Education, 267 F. Supp. 458 (M. D. Ala. 1967); Hawkins v. North Carolina State Board of Education, 11 Race Rel. L. Rep. 745 (W.D.N.C. 1966).

5 Smith v. Allwright, 321 U.S. 649 (1944).

6 Burton v. Wilmington Parking Authority, 365 U.S. 715 (1961).

7 Evans v. Newton, 382 U.S. 296 (1966). For a subsequent case holding that because the park could not be run on a segregated basis as requested in the donor's will, ownership must revert to other heirs, see, Evans v. Abney, 90 S. Ct. 628 (1970).

8 Simkins v. Moses H. Cone Memorial Hospital, 323 F. 2d 959 (4th Cir. 1963), cert. denied, 376 U.S. 938 (1964). Accord, Cypress v. Newport New General and Nonsectarian Hospital Assoc., 392 F. 2d 89 (4th Cir. 1967).

9 For an important case holding Girard College subject to state action, see, Pennsylvania v. Brown, 270 F. Supp. 782 (E.D. Pa. 1967), aff'd 392 F. 2d 120 (3rd Cir. 1968), cert. denied, 391 U.S. 921. Cf. the holding of J. Skelly Wright: "At the outset, one may question whether any school or college can ever be so 'private' as to escape the reach of the Fourteenth Amendment. Institutions of learning are not things of purely private concern.... No one any longer doubts that education is a matter affected with the greatest public interest. And this is true whether it is offered by a public or private institution. Clearly the administrators of a private college are performing a public function. They do the work of the state, often in the place of the state. Does it not follow that they stand in the state's shoes? Reason and authority strongly suggest that the Constitution never sanctions racial discrimination in our schools and colleges, no matter how 'private' they may claim to be." Guillory v. Administrators of Tulane University, 203 F. Supp. 855, 858-59 (E. D. La. 1962), opinion vacated on other grounds, 207 F. Supp. 554, aff'd, 306 F. 2d 489 (5th Cir. 1962).

10 De jure segregation has been held unconstitutional by the courts; de facto segregation, by contrast, has generally not. See, Offerman v. Nitkowski, 378 F. 2d 22 (2nd Cir. 1967); Deal v. Cincinnati Board of Education, 367 F. 2d 55 (6th Cir. 1966), cert. denied, 389 U.S. 847 (1967); Springfield School Committee v. Barksdale, 348 F.2d 261 (1st Cir. 1965). Contra, Blocker v. Board of Education, 226 F. Supp. 208, 229 F. Supp. 709

But it strongly argues that whatever decisions affect public schools would also apply to private schools accepting voucher funds. Thus if a voucher school were found to discriminate unconstitutionally against the admission of minority students, it would be ordered to "desegregate" itself. Alternatively, the transfer of public funds to such a school might be enjoined.[11]

A third remedy might also be available in the case of a discriminatory voucher school.[12] The courts could look not only to the school itself, but to the local or state education agency which adopted the voucher plan. This approach was taken in the Southern voucher cases. Courts there held that if the adoption of a voucher system had been motivated by a desire to further racial discrimination, the entire plan should be enjoined. This approach avoids dealing with private discrimination, for a court sees itself as testing the action of a governmental body (be it state or local). If that action furthers discrimination, the entire program can be voided.

What if a state does not intend to fund racially discriminatory schools under a voucher system, yet the system in fact supports some discriminatory schools? Would the entire program still be voided? While there is little case law which speaks to this point, two trends emerge. First, in testing the "purpose" of the governmental body which adopts a voucher plan, courts have tended to look at the actual or probable effect of the plan.[13] If either would aid discriminatory

---

(E.D.N.Y. 1964); *Branche v. Board of Education*, 204 F. Supp. 150 (E.D.N.Y. 1962). While there is little sign of this distinction changing, it is becoming less important as courts appear more willing to label situations in the North and West as *de jure*. Recently, for example, *de jure* segregation has been found, and held unconstitutional, in Colorado, Illinois, California, and Michigan. *See, Bradley v. Milliken*, Civ. No. 20794 (6th Cir. 1970); *Davis v. School District of Pontiac*, Civ. No. 32392 (E.D. Mich. 1970); *Keynes v. School District No. 2*, 303 F. Supp. 280 (D. Colo. 1969); *United States v. School District 151 of Cook County, Illinois*, 301 F. Supp. 210 (N.D. Ill. 1969); *Crawford v. Board of Education of Los Angeles County*, Civ. No. 822854 (Cal. Sup. Ct. 1970).

11   The extent to which courts will go to prevent any aid going to discriminatory private schools is indicated by the recent ruling in *Green v. Kennedy*, 309 F. Supp. 1127 (D.D.C. 1970). There a three-judge court granted a preliminary injunction against tax benefits (which are traditionally sacrosanct) because they were going to segregated private Mississippi schools.

12   The term "voucher school" or "nonpublic school" is used throughout this article to call attention to the fact that the traditional labeling of schools as public or private is often misleading. The term "public" is applied to colleges even when they charge tuition many people cannot afford; or to academically exclusive high schools even when they have admission requirements few can meet; or to entire school systems even though they refuse to give out information about what they are doing or how well they are doing it. Conversely, the term "private" is applied to schools run by private organizations even when they are open to all applicants on a nondiscriminatory basis, charge no tuition, and willingly provide information about their operation. In other words, definitions have focused too much on *who* runs schools and not enough on *how* they are run.

13   *See, Gomillon v. Lightfoot*, 364 U.S. 339 (1960), in which the Supreme Court considered a law establishing municipal boundaries. On the surface, the law was unob-

schools, then the courts are likely to find that was the intended purpose of the plan, and the entire program would be suspect.

But even if the courts did not find governmental purpose to aid discrimination, they might nonetheless enjoin any program which lacked sufficient safeguards against discrimination. Thus in *Griffin v. State Board of Education*,[14] a federal district court held unconstitutional a state legislated tuition voucher plan, despite arguments that grants to individual schools which discriminated could be stopped without enjoining the entire program. In the words of that court:

> The canvassing and policing of the tuition law to confine its enjoinment to instances [which do not further segregation] would be a Herculean task. It could hardly give full assurance against the abuse of the law. A law may of course survive despite its unacceptable consequences, if the valid portions may be independently enforced. Here, as we see, there can be no such separation and the entire law must go.[15]

The court's language could mean that no voucher plan will ever be acceptable because of the danger of aiding discriminatory schools. More reasonably, however, the decision places a heavy responsibility on any governmental body about to adopt a voucher plan. It must devise one in which the state itself polices discrimination to the satisfaction of the courts.

The Center proposal which includes both a random admissions process for at least half the places in participating schools and state enforcement machinery for detecting and eliminating invidious discrimination in voucher schools is one good approach to the problem. Even if racial discrimination by the state or by individual voucher schools is forbidden, however, a voucher school might, in fact, have a racially segregated student body if students of only one race applied to the school. A state or local agency could adopt a racial balance requirement to prevent this, of course, but such action may not be mandated by the Constitution. Genuine freedom-of-choice plans have not been found unconstitutional except in areas which previously had school systems segregated by law. In those jurisdictions the Court has held freedom-of-choice plans are unconstitutional if there are reasonably available other ways "promising speedier and more effective conversion to a unitary, nonracial school system."[16] In those

---

jectionable. Nonetheless, the Court ruled that if the *effect* of the law was to deprive black citizens of the benefits of municipal residence, including the right to vote in municipal elections, then it was unconstitutional. For a more complete discussion of the role legislative motivation should play in constitutional adjudication, *see*, Ely, "Legislative and Administrative Motivation in Constitutional Law," *Yale Law Journal*, Vol. 79, 1970.

14 *Griffin v. State Board of Education*, 296 F. Supp. 1178 (E.D. Va. 1969).
15 *Ibid.*
16 *Green v. County School Board*, 391 U.S. 430. 441 (1968).

jurisdictions, a voucher plan might not be held constitutional until the courts were satisfied that the dual school system had been abolished.

How big a segregationist "loophole" is the voucher system's reliance on parental choice? If minority parents are assured admission to any school (e.g., if a large portion of the places in any school are allocated randomly among applicants), those who desire integrated schools for their children can make that choice. Some, of course, will not. There will likely be some all-white or all-black schools, a not uncommon situation in the North and the South. Indeed, financial incentives combined with better quality programs, which should attract both black and white students to all schools, may do more than any of the attempts made so far in Northern cities to provide more students with an integrated experience. To suggest that parents might consider educational factors at least as important as racial ones strikes some as ingenuous. But it may be the most pragmatic basis on which to resolve the deepening racial schism in education. Certainly, past practice, where choice has been restricted to the financially favored, is a weak basis on which to judge.

Finally, an analysis of the relationship between voucher schools and the equal protection clause must also consider the extent of the protection provided. Judicial concern for equal educational opportunity has, until now, focused primarily on prohibiting racial discrimination. But other children may need protection too. The rationale of *Brown v. Board of Education*[17] could apply with equal, if not greater force, to poor children as to black children.[18] The extent to which courts will give the same careful attention to poor children, however, remains unclear. Present cases do not extend this far. Proponents of egalitarian voucher systems must, at least for the present, voluntarily build such protection into their plans. Otherwise, they may be disappointed when the courts do not come to the rescue of poor children, even though persuasive legal and educational arguments can be made for such action.

Religion and Vouchers   If misplaced identification of the voucher concept and aid to segregated schools fail to kill the pro-

17 *Brown, op. cit.*
18 *See,* John E. Coons, William H. Clune III, and Stephen D. Sugarman. *Private Wealth and Public Education.* Cambridge: Harvard University Press, 1970; Kirp, "The Poor, the Schools and Equal Protection," *Harvard Educational Review,* 1968, Vol. 38, p. 635; Michelman, "Forward to the Supreme Court Term of 1969: On Protecting the Poor through the Fourteenth Amendment," *Harvard Law Review,* 1969, Vol. 83, p. 7. *Cf.* James Coleman, *et al., Equality of Educational Opportunity.* Washington, D.C.: U.S. Department of Health, Education and Welfare, 1966: "It appears that variations in the facilities and curricula of the schools account for relatively little variation in pupil achievement insofar as this is measured by standard tests.... A pupil's achievement is strongly related to the educational backgrounds and aspirations of the other students in the school...."

posed voucher plans before they are tried, then fallout from the ancient battle over aid to parochial schools could provide the coup de grâce. The temptation is strong to avoid this fight by excluding parochial schools entirely from the first voucher programs. Yet it is conceptually, politically, and perhaps even constitutionally difficult to justify their exclusion from a plan which is supposedly based on the policy of allowing parents more choice in the education of their children.

Unfortunately, while the law on racial discrimination is fairly clear, the constitutionality of aid to parochial schools is very much in flux. Two cases now before the Supreme Court may soon provide clues: *Lemon v. Kurtzman*,[19] in which a three-judge federal district court upheld the Pennsylvania "purchase-of-secular-services" plan of aid to nonpublic schools; and *DiCenso v. Robinson*,[20] in which a three-judge federal court struck down the Rhode Island purchase-of-services plan. If the Court were sweepingly to hold purchase-of-services plans unconstitutional, parochial schools might also be legally excluded from the voucher plan. But since it is likely to rule narrowly, even a decision against purchase-of-services plans will probably not resolve the issue of parochial school participation in a voucher plan.

Traditional case law in the area, unfortunately, leaves much room for speculation. Only two important Supreme Court cases deal directly with aid to parochial schools. In *Everson v. Board of Education*,[21] the Court upheld public payment of the costs of transporting students to parochial as well as to other nonpublic schools. In *Board of Education of Central District No. 1 v. Allen*,[22] the Court similarly upheld the loan of textbooks. *Walz v. Tax Commission*,[23] the most recent Supreme Court pronouncement on church-state issues, is also relevant. Although it dealt with tax exemptions for churches rather than school aid, it proclaimed new church-state guidelines.

In *Walz*, Chief Justice Burger noted, with a pragmatism that will delight some and anger others, that no perfect or absolute separation of church and state is really possible; the very existence of the First Amendment is an involvement of sorts—one which seeks to mark boundaries which avoid excessive entanglement. In past decisions, including the *Allen* textbook case, the First Amendment was interpreted to require that an aid program have: 1. a secular legisla-

---

19 *Lemon v. Kurtzman*, 310 F. Supp. 35 (E. D. Pa. 1969), *prob.juris.noted*, 90 S. Ct. 1354 (1970).
20 *DiCenso v. Robinson*, 316 F. Supp. (D.R.I. 1970), *prob.juris.noted*, 39 U.S.L.W. 3194, Nov. 10, 1970.
21 *Everson v. Board of Education of the Township of Ewing*, 330 U.S. 1 (1947). *See* also, *Quick Bear v. Leupp*, 210 U.S. 50 (1907), a case upholding public funding of parochial schools attended by Indians.
22 *Board of Education of Central District No. 1 v. Allen*, 392 U.S. 236 (1968).
23 *Walz v. Tax Commission of the City of New York*, 90 S. Ct. 1409 (1970).

tive purpose and 2. an effect which neither advances nor inhibits religion. In *Walz*, by contrast, the Supreme Court held that:

> Each value judgment under the Religion Clauses must ... turn on whether particular acts in question are intended to establish or interfere with religious beliefs and practice or have the effect of doing so.[24]

This modified test seems to narrow the range of activities prohibited by the establishment clause. Legislation which "advances" religion is no longer necessarily barred unless it actually helps to "establish" it. Such aids as busing or loaning textbooks are permissible, in the opinion of the Court, for any activity which "realistically" establishes religion can be stopped "while this Court sits."[25] The *Walz* decision seems to make more constitutionally palatable a voucher program directed at improving the quality of secular education in private as well as public schools.

Walz also placed new importance on the need to avoid excessive entanglement of the state in the affairs of the church. Tax exemptions were upheld in *Walz* in part because they involved less entanglement than would taxing churches. But what constitutes excessive entanglement, as one would suspect, was not clarified. According to the Court, the "test is inescapably one of degree." "The questions are whether the involvement is excessive, and whether it is a continuing one calling for official and continuing surveillance leading to an impermissible degree of entanglement."[26]

The traditional approach to aid to parochial schools has attempted to separate the "secular" from the "sectarian." In the *Everson* busing decision, this was relatively easy for no one seriously charged that bus rides were so inherently "permeated" with religiosity that religion was being directly aided. Indirect aid is apparently acceptable if the direct impact is permissible. Otherwise, one faces the problem that any government service or tax reduction frees private funds which might or might not be devoted to religious activity. Thus if providing bus rides to *all* children is itself an acceptable governmental objective, the "savings" from general busing which accrue to parochial schools (or parents) are also acceptable. It is presumably something like a 5 percent tax reduction for all taxpayers, which might eventually result in a greater contribution to religious activities in the form of personal gifts or bequests.

In *Allen*, permeation was more of a problem, for textbooks are not as obviously secular as are bus rides. But the case had come to the Court on a very meager record. On a limited factual basis, the Court found that the books involved were "secular" and upheld the aid.

24 *Ibid.*
25 *Ibid.*
26 *Ibid.*

Many states have recently passed purchase-of-secular-services legislation. This proliferation of aid to religious schools is based on the notion that the state can purchase secular educational services for its children from religious schools. Sponsors argue that the approach is a reasonable extension of the secular-sectarian line drawing embodied in the *Allen* decision.

Whether their argument is right should be decided soon. The *Lemon* and *DiCenso* cases previously mentioned, which both involve such legislation, are now before the Supreme Court. The Pennsylvania plan, tested in *Lemon*, typifies the purchase-of-services approach. It empowers the State Superintendent of Public Instruction to contract for the purchase of "secular educational services" from nonpublic schools in the state. Secular education services are limited by the act to courses in mathematics, modern foreign languages, physical science, and physical education.[27] The decisions implicit in drawing this list are interesting to contemplate, i.e., Latin is out, but so is Greek. Perhaps the Greeks were considered too religious for the educators of Pennsylvania?

In a voucher system the secular-sectarian approach would mean that vouchers cashed by parochial schools would be limited to strictly secular activities. A less onerous approach might require the participating schools to split the school day explicitly between secular and religious activities. This would presumably decrease the state's burden of policing expenditures.

But whatever one concludes as to the educational wisdom of a plan which skews the curriculum of nonpublic schools by limiting aid to courses which are considered religiously "safe," its constitutionality is in doubt for two reasons.

First, the attempt to police such a line may necessarily entangle the state excessively in the affairs of the church in violation of the *Walz* standard. This appears to be the conclusion reached by the three-judge federal district courts which held unconstitutional both the Rhode Island and the Connecticut purchase-of-services laws.[28] There is, however, an even more serious problem with this type of secular-sectarian distinction. Even if successful, it may not sufficiently protect against the establishment of religion forbidden by the First Amendment. Assume for a moment that religious schools did in some satisfactory way separate secular and sectarian activities for the purpose of spending public funds. Suppose the state were to provide schools of one denomination with many times the funds provided to those of another denomination. Even if those funds were only available for expenditure on secular educational activities, most would agree that the state was helping to establish the religion of the favored schools by helping them to attract more students, and therefore, more potential converts.

---

27 Pa. Stat. Ann. Tit. 24, 5601-09 (1968).
28 *DiCenso v. Robinson, op. cit.; Johnson v. Sanders,* Civ. No. 13432 (D. Conn. Oct. 15, 1970).

This argument depends on assuming some correlation between the amount of resources available and the quality of education provided in a school. The truth of this assumption is not self-evident, particularly in light of the Coleman report.[29] A good teacher may be willing to teach for less money than a poor teacher; expensive equipment may not be as important as skilled instruction. But extreme differences in the amount of educational resources available will tend to create differences in the quality of education provided in different schools, if only because it will become more difficult to keep salaries competitive or equipment up-to-date as the relative differences between the resources of schools increase. While not as restrictive as a law requiring attendance at the schools of one particular denomination (or of any denomination as opposed to secular nonpublic schools for that matter) unequal state funding of schools looks suspiciously like unconstitutional establishment of religion. Relevant in this regard is *Sherbert v. Verner*.[30] The Supreme Court there held that withholding unemployment benefits from a Seventh-Day Adventist who refused to work on Saturday contrary to her religious belief unconstitutionally interfered with her religious rights. The Court said:

> The Governmental imposition of such a choice (between giving up unemployment benefits or violating her religious precepts) puts the same kind of burden upon the free exercise of religion as would a fine imposed against appellant for her Sunday worship.[31]

Similarly present purchase-of-services plans place the state in the position of favoring some nonpublic schools while discouraging attendance at others because the plans fail to relate funding to enrollment. In Pennsylvania, for example, statistics for the first year of the program reveal some schools received more than ten times as many funds for each child enrolled than other schools.[32] Such a disparity must violate the neutrality in religious matters mandated by the Constitution.

But what alternatives are there to the pitfalls of trying to separate the secular from the sectarian? Not surprisingly, we think that the voucher system is one alternative. There are two constitutional arguments for allowing parochial schools to participate in voucher programs. First, in a voucher system money is transferred to parents who are then permitted to transfer the funds to schools; this may mean that the funds are no longer subject to the constraints of the establishment clause. Alternatively, even if the religion clauses of the

---

29 *See*, Coleman, *op. cit.*
30 *Sherbert v. Verner*, 374 U.S. 398 (1963).
31 *Ibid.*
32 Pennsylvania Office of Aid to Nonpublic Schools, An Analysis of Significant Data (1969).

Constitution do apply to voucher funds, the state remains neutral if it provides roughly equivalent support to the education of a child whether or not the child attends a religious or nonreligious nonpublic school.

The first argument is appealing on its face and gains plausibility from such programs as the G. I. Bill. Under the bill thousands of veterans used government funds not only to attend church-related schools, but for seminary training at that—presumably because the G. I.'s rather than the state chose which school would be "aided."[33]

Other analogies have been proposed. Would it be unconstitutional to support the religious education of children with money provided to parents under family assistance plans or a negative income tax? Would anyone argue that the faithful parishioner violates the Constitution when Social Security payments find their way, at least in part, to the collection plate on the Sabbath? Probably not, for the choice is private and personal; the government is in no way involved in the allocation decision.

The difficulty with this reasoning is that the state is still involved to a certain extent in any voucher program. It requires, for example, that funds be expended only on schools—people cannot choose to use the vouchers entirely at their will. Indeed, the state may place other restrictions on which schools are eligible to cash vouchers, such as the restrictions on admissions embodied in the Center's proposal. With these strings riding with the vouchers, it is more difficult to argue that they somehow become entirely "private" once "given" to parents. Furthermore, in the area of racial discrimination, courts have not hesitated to overlook procedural distinctions in arguing that constitutional limitations apply even though funds are channeled through "private" hands in the form of vouchers. Perhaps racial equality is inherently subject to more stringent constitutional protection and scrutiny than religious rights, but the distinction may be hard to maintain.

The second argument, which might be termed the neutral funding argument, rests on the notion that the state expends no more to educate a given child in a religious nonpublic school than it would expend to educate the same child in a secular nonpublic school.

Isn't this the same argument parochial schools have been trying to make—with notable lack of success—for years? No. For one thing, it is not an argument that the state *must* fund nonpublic schools. Rather, it is an extension of the doctrine that the judiciary should overrule legislative judgments only when a constitutional principle is clearly violated. If a state legislature has decided that the value of funding *all* nonpublic schools to improve the quality of educational opportunity available to all children outweighs possible establishment

33 72 Stat. 1177 (1958), 38 U.S.C. 1620. Approximately 36,000 veterans used the G. I. Bill to pay for training as Protestant ministers.

dangers, that judgment should not be lightly overturned. This is especially true in light of the Supreme Court's apparent willingness to reject only those programs which "realistically" establish religion.

But what of the prayers and other religious activities that may go on in parochial schools which receive funds? Isn't this a clear violation of the cases outlawing prayers or Bible reading? No. Those cases all arose with regard to practices in the public schools, which children of many religions are forced to attend. In a voucher system as long as secular public (and perhaps secular non-public) schools are open to any child, then no child will be in a parochial school except at the choice of his parents. Indeed, past Supreme Court decisions restricting prayers in public schools rested in part on the fact that parents were still free to choose a religious education for their children. In the words of Mr. Justice Brennan:

> Attendance at the public schools has never been compulsory. Parents remain morally and constitutionally free to choose the academic environment in which they wish their children to be educated. In my judgment, the First Amendment forbids the State to inhibit that freedom of choice by diminishing the attractiveness of either alternative—either by restricting the liberty of the private schools to inculcate whatever values they wish, or by jeopardizing the freedom of the public schools from private or sectarian pressures.[34]

Absent public regulation or subsidy, poor families cannot exercise this theoretical freedom of choice. A voucher plan, in this sense, does nothing more than extend to all families the same opportunity to make a religious choice which was previously available only to the relatively affluent.

But even if it is constitutional to allow parents to send their children to publicly subsidized parochial schools, does it not violate the constitutional rights of other taxpayers to make them bear the cost of that subsidy? Two arguments suggest not. First, as long as the state spends no more to educate the child at the parochial school than it would to educate the child in a public school, the taxpayer is not shouldering an unconstitutional religious burden. Without public aid, most children in parochial schools will soon seek admittance to the public system, at perhaps even greater cost to the taxpayers. Secondly, even if aid to parochial schools nevertheless infringes in some way upon the religious rights of taxpayers, that infringement may be less than the infringement of freedom which no aid causes to families who are thereby kept from enrolling their children in parochial schools. The conflicting interests may require balancing, as in other difficult constitutional areas, such as free speech. The balance may well favor aid once an important secular purpose, such as raising the quality of secular education in all schools, is added to the scales.

---

34 *Abington School District v. Schempp*, 372 U.S. at 242 (concurring opinion).

In summary, the fate of participation by religious schools in voucher programs may be determined by the position adopted by the Supreme Court with regard to purchase-of-services legislation. There are several important ways, however, in which voucher plans appear more in keeping with the fundamental policies embodied in the religion clauses than do existing purchase-of-services laws. Therefore, the constitutionality of the parochial school participation in voucher plans will probably remain unresolved until a specific constitutional test of vouchers occurs. In the meantime, educational policy and state laws should guide decisions on this matter.[35]

Quality In Education   Critics of the voucher plan also charge that it may lower the quality of education. They claim the voucher plan would, on the one hand, allow fly-by-night schools to open and flourish. On the other hand, it would allegedly drain the most talented students from the public schools, leaving them only the most difficult children. While these complaints are not the most consistent charges ever raised, they point to two potential problem areas.

First, supporting nonpublic schools could lead to the exodus of the most talented, or the most wealthy, from the public system unless strong guarantees of open admissions are enforced in nonpublic as well as public schools. The restrictions on racial discrimination discussed earlier are important but incomplete safeguards. It is equally important to prevent nonpublic schools from arbitrarily denying entrance to poor students or to those with learning problems. Because the protections of the Fourteenth Amendment are unlikely to go far enough, administrative or statutory guarantees are necessary. The Center proposal that any school should allocate at least one half of its open places *randomly* among the students *who apply* to that school is one approach. Consideration should also be given to possible frustration of open admissions require-

---

35 For an example of more restrictive state provisions, *see,* New York Constitution, Art. 11, 3 (known as the Blaine Amendment): "Neither the state nor any subdivision thereof shall use its property or credit or any public money, or authorize or permit either to be used, directly or indirectly, in aid of maintenance, other than for examination or inspection, of any school or institution of learning wholly or in part under the control or direction of any religious denomination, or in which any denominational tenet or doctrine is taught, but the legislature may provide for the transportation of children to and from any school or institution of learning." But the textbook program upheld in *Allen* was also upheld against this provision of the New York State Constitution. For discussion of the theory that just as the free exercise clause may limit the application of the establishment clause, now that it had been applied to the states, so it may also limit state constitutional provisions which are more restrictive of free exercise rights, *see,* A.M. Bickel. *The Supreme Court and the Idea of Progress.* New York: Harper & Row, 1970; Drinan, "*Public Aid to Parochial Schools,*" 75 *Case and Comment* 13 (1970). *Cf. Mulkey v. Reitman,* 387 U.S. 369 (1967).

ments that could arise if nonpublic schools could arbitrarily suspend or expel "undesirable" students. The Center proposal suggests that all students should be entitled to at least the same due process protections in suspension or expulsion proceedings that they are accorded in the public system. Appropriate legislation can accomplish these results. With genuine open admissions, public schools should not be at a disadvantage with regard to serving students of all needs and abilities.

The problem of maintaining quality in nonpublic schools remains. Financial hucksterism should be relatively easy to avoid. If nothing else, voucher funds might be issued at intervals during the year, thereby preventing a school from opening, collecting all of its funds, and disappearing into the night.

But what of educational hucksterism? First, whether or not public funds are provided, states have a clear right to regulate all nonpublic schools. As the Supreme Court explained in *Allen*:

> Since *Pierce* [*v. Society of Sisters*], a substantial body of case law has confirmed the power of the States to insist that attendance at private schools, if it is to satisfy state compulsory-attendance laws, be at institutions which provide minimum hours of instruction, employ teachers of specified training, and cover prescribed subjects of instruction. [These] cases were a sensible corollary of *Pierce v. Society of Sisters:* if the State must satisfy its interest in secular education through the instrument of private schools, it has a proper interest in the manner in which those schools perform their secular education function.[36]

In exercising this right to regulate all schools, public and nonpublic alike, many states demand certification of nonpublic school teachers. Others specifically define required courses, or various measures of equivalence between nonpublic and public school instruction.[37]

Indeed, the legal precedent for state control of nonpublic schools is so clear that the real danger is not lack of regulation but overzealous regulation. The end result could be to turn nonpublic schools into carbon copies of the most restricted public schools unless freedom for diversity and from unnecessary regulation is carefully protected.

Relevant legal precedent is again available. In *Pierce v. Society of Sisters*, a decision which might be viewed as the magna charta of nonpublic schools, the Supreme Court struck down an Oregon statute which would have required all children to attend public schools. It held that "the fundamental theory of lib-

---

36 *Board of Education of Central District No. 1 v. Allen, op. cit.*
37 For a detailed history of state regulatory statutes, *see,* Elson, "State Regulation of Non-public Schools: The Legal Fraamework" in Donald Erickson. *Public Controls for Non-Public Schools.* Chicago: University of Chicago Press, 1969.

erty upon which all governments in this Union repose excludes any general power of the State to standardize its children by forcing them to accept instruction from public teachers." [38]

Similarly in *Meyer v. Nebraska*, the Court struck down a Nebraska statute which prohibited teaching any language but English to anyone who had not passed the eighth grade. It held that the statute violated the teacher's "right thus to teach and the right of parents to engage him so to instruct their children."[39] Finally, in *Farrington v. Tokushige*,[40] the Court struck down a Hawaii statute which both taxed and heavily regulated the Japanese foreign language schools. The Court found that the law deprived parents of a fair opportunity to procure for their children instruction which they thought important.

In a voucher system parents are the responsible arbiters of quality. While the state should certainly continue to be vigilant in denying funds to educationally dangerous schools, the real danger is that the state may instead become a vigilante driving out diversity in nonpublic schools. Overzealous effort to "protect children" and their parents from their mistakes could destroy what little diversity now exists.

In Conclusion In this examination of some major legal aspects of a voucher plan, three characteristic relationships between legal and educational policies have emerged. With racial segregation, legal constraints and educational wisdom run parallel. In church-state matters, federal law remains unclear. State law is often restrictive and may hamper the free play of educational choice. In the regulation of quality, there is a wide variety of choices. Power to regulate is clear, and the critical issue is how state and local officials will use their considerable authority.

The law does erect firm barriers to some types of voucher plans. Plans aimed at furthering racial discrimination, for example, would be forbidden. But for the most part, courts have avoided educational policy-making, stepping in only in those instances, such as racial discrimination, where efforts at self-regulation have failed. This is as it should be, for the other side of imposing apparently desirable principles by judicial fiat is a loss of flexibility, of maneuverability in shaping the education of our children and ourselves. It also means that difficult issues of religion, of quality, and ultimately the way in which we finance education will not be resolved by judges; they remain for us to decide.

38 *Pierce v. Society of Sisters,* 268 U.S. 510, 535 (1925).
39 *Meyer v. Nebraska,* 262 U.S. 390, 400 (1923).
40 *Farrington v. Tokushige,* 273 U.S. 284 (1927).

Vouchers: The End of Public Education?

George La Noue, the editor of this volume, is
associate professor of politics and education at
Teachers College, Columbia University. In
this essay, by examining the political and
legal assumptions of regulation, he challenges
the belief that the regulated voucher can avoid
the problems of the unregulated voucher.
Professor La Noue further criticizes the
concept of the voucher "experiment."

George La Noue, "The Politics of Education," Teachers College Record, Vol. 73, No. 2
(December 1971), pp. 304-319.

George R. La Noue

In his essay in the tenth anniversary issue of the *Saturday Review's* educational supplement, Peter Schrag formulates a question that has been lurking on the edges of much of the contemporary debate about schools. Have we, he asks, reached the "end of the impossible dream" of public education?[1]

Schrag thinks we have. The time has come, he argues, to admit that the educational reforms of the sixties have been of little consequence and the public school system itself has failed. How do we know public schools have failed? For Schrag, like other educational romantics, the question need not be taken seriously in quantitative terms. He writes:

> Evidence? Is it necessary again to cite statistics, dropout rates, figures on black and white children who go to college (or finish high school), comparisons of academic success between rich and poor kids, college attendance figures for slums and suburbs?[2]

Actually, of course, the statistics are not that one-sided. For example, college board scores show that the public schools in the sixties did accomplish their post-Sputnik mandate of producing students with higher mathematical, scientific, and technological skills. Progress has been made with the more intractable problem of racial equality of opportunity. In 1960, the median school year completed by nonwhites in the United States was 10.8; by whites, 12.3. By 1968 the gap had narrowed to 12.2 for nonwhites and 12.6 for whites.[3] Furthermore, the number of black students in colleges doubled between 1964 and 1969, and black youngsters are now more likely to be enrolled in preschool programs than are whites.[4]

1 Peter Schrag, "End of the Impossible Dream," *Saturday Review*, September 19, 1970, p. 68.
2 *Ibid.*
3 U.S. Department of Labor and U.S. Department of Commerce, "Recent Trends in Social and Economic Conditions of Negroes in the United States," Current Population Reports Series, p. 23, No. 26, BCS Report No. 347, July, 1968.
4 "Blacks in School at a Higher Rate," *New York Times*, October 11, 1970; Robert L. Jacobson, "Education Gains by Poor Called Revolutionary," *The Chronicle of Higher Education*, March 10, 1969, Vol. III, No. 13, p. 1.

It is currently fashionable to dismiss these gains as too slow or even irrelevant. None of the very real problems that exist in public schools should be minimized. But if we become so cavalier in our criticism that we do not notice the achievements that have been made, the probability of successful diagnosis for further reform is diminished. Nevertheless, after a decade of intense concern about schools on the part of social scientists, it is still almost impossible to document the patterns of strength and weakness in school systems in terms that are policy-relevant. We have neither the data nor the conceptual models that would permit conclusions about relative achievement of school systems. If one takes into account their various socioeconomic and political contexts, who can say that the New York public school system is better or worse than those in Chicago, Los Angeles, or Atlanta.

A part of the problem is poor information. The public school establishment has been enormously successful in resisting pressures to gather and distribute data that could be used to challenge it. On the other hand, the educational research establishment, with its built-in incentive to discover failure which justifies ever more research, has not done much to develop comparative models which could add objectivity to the evaluation. Consequently, the debate has been dominated by the educational romantics whose rhetoric fits the current intellectual mood of condemning all American institutions, the Presidency, the Congress, the judiciary, state and local governments, the military, medicine, business, unions, universities, etc., etc., as failures. Such an undiscriminating mood may be personally cathartic, and many of us indulge in it at times, but no rational public policy can be based on it. Both the achievements and the problems of public education should be recognized. Any realistic strategy for educational reform must be prepared to deal with both.

There is also a more subtle problem. Schrag argues that our culture is changing so rapidly that Americans may no longer be able to define educational success. In losing our consensus about educational goals, we also inevitably undermine the basis of a public school system. Schrag believes that the problem with public schools is not, as others have suggested, that they are politically unaccountable, but that, to the contrary, they do "precisely what most Americans expect." He insists:

> Any single, universal public institution—and especially one as sensitive as the public school—is the product of a social quotient verdict. It elevates the lowest common denominator of desires, pressures, and demands into the highest public virtue. It cannot afford to offend any sizeable community group, be it the American Legion, the B'nai B'rith, or the NAACP. Nor can it become a subversive enterprise that is designed to encourage children to ask real questions about race or sex or social justice or the emptiness and joys of life.[5]

5 Schrag, *op. cit.*, p. 70.

One can agree that some schools unnecessarily inhibit controversial ideas, but Schrag appears to advocate a kind of pluralism that is really cultural segregation. Consequently he concludes that public education is no longer possible or desirable.

The solution Schrag proposes is a dismantling of the public school system by adopting a voucher system. The fundamental question in the politics of education today, then, is not curricular reform or community control, but whether the public school system itself should be abandoned or modified in favor of some new kind of relationship between parent, government, and school. Schrag would substitute consumer accountability between parents and schools for the existing political accountability. He writes: "Separate schools, accountable not to public vote and citizen support but only to their clients, may be immune to such [conformist] pressures; they will have to make their way on the basis of performance." The implications of such a change for public schools are enormous. As Christopher Jencks expressed it in his early writing on vouchers, before he became a more cautious political manager of the concept:

> Either tuition grants or management contracts to private organizations would, of course, "destroy the public school system as we know it." When one thinks of the remarkable past achievements of public education in America, this may seem a foolish step. But we must not allow the memory of past achievements to blind us to present failures. Nor should we allow the rhetoric of public school men to obscure the issue. It is natural for public servants to complain about private competition. But if the terms of the competition are reasonable, there is every reason to suppose that it is healthy. Without it, both public and private enterprises have a way of ossifying. And if, as some fear, the public schools could not survive in open competition with private ones, then perhaps they *should* not survive.[6]

The Concept of Public and Private   Like most other voucher writers,[7] Schrag does not define the difference between public and private schools very precisely. The imagery is clear, however. Public schools are monolithic, while private schools are more flexible and innovative. Establishing definitions and the facts of the matter are critical elements in the policy decision.

---

6 Christopher Jencks, "Is the Public School Obsolete?" *The Public Interest*, Winter, 1965, p. 27.

7 Jencks reconceptualizes the terms public and private to mean that public schools must be open to all (they may not even have geographical or academic requirements), must not charge tuition or "refuse to give anyone information about what they are doing, how well they are doing it, and whether children are getting what their parents want." *Education Vouchers*. Cambridge, Mass.: Center for the Study of Public Policy, December 1970, p. 13. This definition may be useful to advance a normative argument, but it has no legal or historic validity. There are probably no existing schools that would meet all of the tests to be called public.

To consider private schools first, about 5,600,000 children, or about 11 percent of the total elementary and secondary population, attend schools traditionally classified as private. Almost 90 percent of these children are in Catholic schools; another 5 percent are in Protestant and Jewish schools; while the remaining 5 percent attend secular private or prep schools. Although it may be difficult for a Bostonian or New Yorker to believe, most nonpublic schools are conventional parochial or prep schools. The kind of "flexible, innovative" private school they envision is only a tiny minority, quite insignificant statistically (about 1 percent) in terms of national school enrollment. Given these facts, whether private schools when compared school for school with public schools are more flexible and innovative remains to be proven.

The public school "monolith" turns out to be divided into more than 16,000 local governing districts. Although public schools reflect a generally similar curriculum (most of the state laws establishing curricular requirements cover private schools too), it is difficult to think of other generalizations that can be made on a national level. The governing and taxing patterns of public schools, their size, constituencies, employment practices, quality, and innovativeness vary as much as the character of American life itself.

Indeed, there is only one common bond between the public schools of Jackson, Michigan, and Jackson, Mississippi, of Portland, Oregon, and Portland, Maine. Public schools are all bound by judicial interpretations of the federal Constitution, while private schools are exempt. While public schools may generally be larger, more bureaucratic, and more unionized than private schools, none of these characteristics is inherent or even uniform. The legal obligation to obey the freedom of religion, speech, petition, and assembly clauses of the First Amendment and the due process and equal protection clauses of the Fourteenth Amendment, however, is now universally binding.

Before the 1940s, the legal distinction between public and private schools made little functional difference. The Supreme Court studiously avoided becoming involved in what were considered local educational matters. But in 1943, in a dramatic reversal of an earlier opinion, the Court decided that public school authorities could not force children of Jehovah's Witnesses to salute the flag.[8] The modern era of judicial educational policy making had begun.

Five years later, Edward Corwin, then the dean of American constitutional scholars, wrote a satirical essay, "The Supreme Court as a National School Board," to express his distaste for this trend.[9] The Court itself has shown some hesitation about its new role, but it has acted nevertheless. While striking down a state prohibition against teaching evolution, the Court declared:

8 *West Virginia State Board of Education v. Barnette*, 319 U.S. 624 (1943).
9 *Law and Contemporary Problems*, Vol. XIV, Winter, 1949, p. 3.

Judicial interposition in the operation of the public school systems of the Nation raises problems requiring care and restraint. Our courts, however, have not failed to apply the First Amendment's mandate in our educational system where essential to safeguard the fundamental values of freedom of speech and inquiry and of belief. By and large, public education in our Nation is committed to the control of state and local authorities. Courts do not and cannot intervene in the resolution of conflicts which arise in the daily operation of school systems and which do not directly and sharply implicate basic constitutional values. On the other hand, "The vigilant protection of constitutional values is nowhere more vital than in the community of the American Schools."[10]

Professor Corwin's title has turned out to be prophetic. In case after case in the last thirty years, the federal courts have established themselves as a major determiner of public school policy. Today all public schools are bound by four principles which the courts have extracted from the First and Fourteenth Amendments: nondiscrimination, academic freedom, equality of opportunity, and public accountability. The courts are still developing their interpretations of these doctrines and some have met with widespread resistance, but these principles may be regarded as the constitutional framework within which all public schools will eventually have to operate.

nondiscrimination

| public accountability | | academic freedom |

equality of opportunity

Although the full impact of judicial intervention has yet to be felt, the principles already established are of considerable consequence. In 1954, the Court struck down the doctrine of racially separate-but-equal schools that was the controlling public policy for over 40 percent of the nation's school children in seventeen states and the District of Columbia.[11] Enforcement of that decision has been slow and painful, but de jure segregation is now dead and the courts are whittling away at the boundaries of de facto segregation. In addition, the courts have challenged sexual discrimination and stand as guardians against religious discrimination.

In the area of academic freedom the courts have moved to protect teachers

10 *Epperson v. State of Arkansas,* 393 U.S. 97 (1969).
11 *Brown v. Board of Education,* 347 U.S. 483 (1954).

from invidious loyalty oaths[12] and have given them the right to criticize official school policy without retaliation.[13] They have prohibited public schools from engaging in overt indoctrination[14] and have defined them as neither the "partisan (n)or the enemy of any class, creed, party or faction."[15] Most dramatic has been the judicial expansion of student rights. Only a few years ago, *in loco parentis*, a doctrine which permitted public schools to act as arbitrarily as families in dealing with children, was the acknowledged rule. Today the courts are establishing a whole new set of procedural due process rights for students in disciplinary cases.[16] In decisions like *Tinker v. Des Moines*,[17] which ruled that public school students had the right to wear armbands protesting war if they did not otherwise disrupt the school, the Supreme Court has altered the concept of the right of student expression all over the country. One consequence in New York is the Board of Education's new student handbook which, if enforced, will give public school students more rights than most private college students now enjoy.

Protecting equality of educational opportunity has proved more difficult for the Court. This has been caused, not by a lack of constitutional justification or judicial commitment, but rather by the difficulty of creating a workable and enforceable definition of the concept.[18] So far the Supreme Court has avoided the simplistic and rigid interpretation that the equal protection clause requires equal spending per student,[19] but in *Hobson v. Hansen*,[20] a federal court has ordered the Washington, D.C. school board to shuffle its resources to improve the facilities available to poor children. The recent decision by a federal court of appeals requiring the town of Shaw, Mississippi, to provide equal public services to each section of the town surely has implications for education.[21]

Judicial articulation of public accountability is the least developed of the four principles. The courts have, however, applied the one-man-one-vote rule to school board elections and have intervened to see that rules of community consultation and adequate disclosure be followed.[22] Particularly as urban schools

12 For a discussion of recent cases, see E. Edmund Reutter, Jr. and Robert R. Hamilton. *The Law of Public Education.* Mineola, New York: The Foundation Press, 1970.
13 *Pickering v. Board of Education*, 391 U.S. 563 (1968).
14 In addition to *West Virginia State Board of Education v. Barnette* and *Epperson v. Arkansas, Engel v. Vitale*, 370 U.S. 421 (1962), and *School District of Abington Township, Pa. v. Schempp*, 374 U.S. 203 (1963) stand for this principle.
15 *West Virginia State Board of Education v. Barnette, op. cit.*
16 There is a substantial literature on this subject. One of the best pieces is C. Michael Abbott, "Demonstrations, Dismissals, Due Process and the High School: An Overview," *The School Review*, June, 1969, pp. 128-142.
17 *Tinker v. Des Moines Independent Community School District*, 393 U.S. 503 (1969).
18 See, for example, the discussions in Charles U. Daly, ed., *The Quality of Inequality*. Chicago: The University of Chicago Press, 1968.
19 *McInnis v. Ogilvie*, 394 U.S. 322 (1969).
20 *Hobson v. Hansen*, 269 F. Supp. 401 (1967).
21 *New York Times*, February 2, 1971, p. 1.
22 For a discussion of the impact of judicial decisions on school board operating procedure, see Reutter and Hamilton, *op. cit.*

develop new decentralized or federalized patterns of government, we can expect to see courts intervene to protect public access and information.

This brief summary is barely adequate to describe the scope and import of judicial intervention into educational policy, but it does serve to indicate the constitutional framework within which public schools must legally operate. Public schools are bound by this framework through the Fourteenth Amendment which declares that no state "shall make or enforce any law which shall abridge the privileges or immunities of citizens of the United States; nor shall any State deprive any person of life, liberty, or property, without due process of law; nor deny to any person within its jurisdiction the equal protection of the laws." Public schools are considered to be extensions of state governments or to involve "state action," and are therefore affected by the Fourteenth Amendment. Private institutions, if they are really private, are not considered to involve "state action" and are legally exempt from constitutional restrictions. For example, a church need not follow one-man-one-vote in electing its leaders or due process in disciplining its members. However, determining the legal definition of a private constitutionally-exempt institution is quite complicated.

When the Southern states began to devise legal maneuvers to confirm "private" status on previously public institutions, or began to channel public functions through traditionally private institutions, the federal courts expanded the concept of "state action" to prohibit further discrimination. Whether a particular private institution may involve state action is still subject to case-by-case litigation. But, in general, a "private" institution may involve state action, and thus be subject to constitutional sanctions, if it is substantially regulated by the state; if it accepts substantial amounts of state funds; or if it serves a public function. In addition, a "private" institution that significantly affects interstate commerce may be subject to legislation based on that constitutional clause.

These legal rules raise a complicated problem for voucher advocates. Are schools that participate in tax-supported voucher plans involved in "state action"? If so, wouldn't that mean that parochial schools would have to give up sectarian courses in religion (*McCollum v. Illinois*)[23] and prayer and Bible-reading (*Abington Township v. Schempp*)[24] as public schools have had to do? Would a military academy be bound by the *Tinker v. Des Moines*[25] armband rule? Would private schools be involved in rulings like *Hobson v. Hansen*[26] against racial imbalance and expenditure inequalities?

If the answer to these questions is yes, then most private schools would refuse to participate in a voucher plan. If the answer is no, then substantial numbers of parents might use vouchers to buy education outside the constitutional framework. The questions are critical in understanding the effect vouchers might have

23 *Illinois ex. rel. McCollum v. Board of Education*, 333 U.S. 203 (1948).
24 *School District of Abington Township, Pa. v. Schempp, op. cit.*
25 *Tinker v. Des Moines Independent Community School District, op. cit.*
26 *Hobson v. Hansen, op. cit.*

on American education. The answers turn on the type of voucher being considered.

Types of Vouchers   There is no one voucher plan. Vouchers have been proposed in about as many sizes and shapes as there are educational ideologies. The first of the modern voucher concepts was created by Father Virgil C. Blum, a Jesuit political scientist at Marquette University. In his book *Freedom of Choice in Education*,[27] he used the traditional Catholic social philosophy of subsidiarity to develop the concept that values in a schools' curriculum and culture should be totally determined by parents. To promote this doctrine, Blum had earlier founded Citizens for Educational Freedom, a predominantly lay Catholic organization which has attracted adherents from other conservative religious groups.

CEF has consistently supported vouchers as the device that would provide the most tax funds for parochial schools with the least amount of public controls. It was Father Blum who first developed the analogy, still used by voucher proponents, between education vouchers and the GI Bill and social security payments. The analogy is not completely accurate, since, unlike most government programs, the beneficiaries in these programs have established their individual claim by prior service (GI Bill) or by prepayment of insurance premiums (Social Security). The money thus "belongs" to them and they can spend it without constitutional restriction. Veterans, for example, used GI payments to attend seminaries; nobody knows how social security payments are spent. Even if the sources and rationale of these two government programs are not analogous, CEF has found them to be a convenient model for the kind of educational voucher it advocates. The CEF voucher is unregulated—the recipient school need meet no additional statutory or constitutional standards—and noncompensatory—a parent's income would not affect the size of the voucher.

CEF has operated as a pressure group in the United States for about fifteen years. It has not had much success in obtaining vouchers, although some textbook and bus transportation battles have been won. Ironically, its greatest victory, a purchase-of-services law obtained through a coalition with the White Citizens' Councils in Louisiana, was its most short-lived. The Louisiana State Supreme Court struck down the law before it could be implemented on the grounds that that kind of aid to private schools violated separation of church and state.[28]

Another contribution to the development of vouchers was made by Milton Friedman, the University of Chicago economist, in his book *Capitalism and*

27 Virgil C. Blum. *Freedom of Choice in Education*. New York: Macmillan, 1958.
28 *Seegers v. Parker*, 256 La. 1039 (1970). [This article was written before *Serrano v. Priest*, which establishes new principles of educational equality, was decided.]

Freedom.[29] In that general exposition of the virtues of marketplace competition as a device for creating choice and diversity, education is treated as merely one of the public services (hospitals, libraries, parks, etc.) that might be better rendered by private enterprise. Later, in magazine articles, Professor Friedman focused on the idea of an educational voucher, but his original commitment to the unregulated "free enterprise" voucher remained.

In contrast, the most recent proponents of vouchers, Christopher Jencks and his colleagues at the Harvard Center for the Study of Public Policy, and John B. Coons, William H. Clune III, and Stephen D. Sugarman in their book *Private Wealth and Public Education*[30] advocate only regulated vouchers. Indeed, Jencks concedes that "an unregulated voucher system could be the most serious setback for the education of disadvantaged children in the history of the United States."[31]

The Coons et al. proposal is a sophisticated and sensitive attempt to give families a choice, not only about the style of education they prefer, but also about the amount of family resources they wish to commit to education. Schools charging different levels of tuition would be established. The amount of the voucher would depend on the family income and the cost of the school. A high income family choosing a high cost school would receive a relatively much smaller voucher than a poor family choosing a low cost school.

The most publicized proposal, however, comes from the Harvard Center's report that was the result of an Office of Economic Opportunity grant of $193,000 to study vouchers. Since Christopher Jencks, the principal author, had already committed himself in print to vouchers, the final report might have seemed anti-climactic. However, the Jencks volume performs a very useful purpose in outlining alternative voucher models (some eleven versions are discussed). It confronts in a candid manner the possible inequalitarian and anti-civil libertarian results of vouchers. Jencks and company clearly reject the concept of unregulated vouchers and develop instead a highly sophisticated set of regulations which recipient schools would have to follow. The major restrictions on a voucher school would be that it:

1. Accept a voucher as full payment of tuition.
2. Accept any applicant so long as it had vacant places.
3. If it had more applicants than places, fill at least half these places by picking applicants randomly and fill the other half in such a way as not to discriminate against ethnic minorities.

29 Milton Friedman. *Capitalism and Freedom*. Chicago: The University of Chicago Press, 1962.
30 John B. Coons, William H. Clune III, Stephen D. Sugarman. *Private Wealth and Public Education*. Cambridge, Mass.: Harvard University Press, 1970.
31 *Education Vouchers*. Center for the Study of Public Policy, *op. cit.*, p. 17.

4. Accept uniform standards established by the Educational Voucher Agency regarding suspension and expulsion of students.
5. Agree to make a wide variety of information about its facilities, teachers, program, and students available to the EVA and to the public.
6. Maintain accounts of money received and disbursed in a form that would allow both parents and the EVA to determine whether a school operated by a board of education was getting the resources to which it was entitled on the basis of its vouchers, whether a school operated by a church was being used to subsidize other church activities, and whether a school operated by a profit-making corporation was siphoning off excessive amounts to the parent corporation.
7. Meet existing state requirements for private schools regarding curriculum, staffing, and the like.[32]

The Office of Economic Opportunity, in its competition with the Office of Education for educational influence, has responded favorably to the Jencks report and has announced its intention to fund several five-to-eight-year experiments. The effort has not gone well. Although federal money is usually a desirable commodity, school systems have been turning OEO down at an unprecedented rate. Indeed, the difficulty of fitting vouchers into local and state laws plus the size of the political opposition may mean that widespread experiments will prove impossible.[33]

On the intellectual circuit, however, vouchers are the hottest item going, and the idea must be taken seriously. Much of the debate has been dominated by considerations of ideology and vested interest, but there is the beginning of a careful critique of the plan on its own terms, with attention being focused on the adequacy of specific regulations on voucher schools. For example, neither the Jencks nor the Coons plan prohibits voucher schools from discrimination in the hiring of teachers. Not only is this a practical problem in the coming era of teacher surplus, but it is obvious that if a school discriminates rigorously enough in selecting its staff, it can discourage "undesirable" students from even applying. Under those circumstances, the careful lottery and dismissal procedures are meaningless. Nor is either plan specific about the use of academic qualifications or dress codes (an expensive school uniform, for example) to restrict enrollment. The alternatives available to a private school that wanted to restrict its enrollment are almost limitless, and perhaps no voucher system can fully cope with them.

---

32 *Ibid.*, p. 15.
33 Ironically, the major political consequence of the speculation about vouchers has been to reestablish the pre-ESEA, antiprivate school aid coalition of public schools, Protestant, Jewish, and civil liberties agencies.

The Regulation of Vouchers Assuming for the moment the adequacy and good faith of the Jencks regulations, can they be enforced? For most of the voucher writers, the marketplace's ability to regulate competition and to produce consumer sovereignty is axiomatic. Adam Smith, not Ralph Nader, is their prophet, and their faith in the virtues of the market is in today's terms almost singular. But which of the great American industries would be a suitable model for the educational marketplace? The "free enterprise" transportation industry? Lockheed or Penn Central? How about the medical industry, now financed in part by Medicare vouchers, which do not seem to have done much to improve the overall health of Americans or even the fiscal solvency of hospitals, though some doctors are doing very well? Or perhaps that sector of education most based on free enterprise—correspondence and trade schools—is the model?

The point is that marketplace analogies do not fit well to the educational world. In the first place, public schools are not a noncompetitive monopoly like the postal service. They are highly decentralized and they do compete, both with private schools, which enroll 15 to 35 percent of the students in most cities, and with each other. (There is, incidentally, no research which shows that public schools are "better" in cities where the greatest competition with private schools exists. Because of the "drainoff" of the middle class in these cities, I suspect the reverse is more likely true.) City schools also compete against suburban schools and with each other for appropriations, teachers, special projects, and status as well as in extracurricular activities.

Competition in the private school sector does not correspond to market theory either. With the possible exception of the housing industry, most profit-making firms will sell their products to anyone with cash or credit regardless of his race, religion, social background, manners, intelligence, or skills. Private schools, however, generally prefer to be exclusive based on one or more of the above factors. They do not view increasing their share of the market in the same way corporations do. This severely limits the possibility of consumer accountability. Although there is no research on the matter, the most plausible generalization is that the more desirable the private school, the less the parental accountability.

The Harvard study is aware of the limitations of the market as regulator, however, and it proposes several devices to skew the market in liberal directions. First, the preferred voucher would be compensatory, providing perhaps twice as many dollars for disadvantaged children. One can make a case that it costs more to educate these children, and since OEO will control the experiments, one can imagine that the vouchers will actually be compensatory. But eventually vouchers will have to be funded by state and local legislatures. Nothing in their history (certainly not their distribution of Title I Elementary and Secondary Education Act money) warrants optimism about their compensatory proclivities. Almost all of the voucher schemes that have been taken seriously by the states thus far have been only mildly compensatory at best.

Secondly, voucher schools would be forbidden to charge amounts in addition to the voucher aid and, if oversubscribed, would have to choose at least half of their students through lottery. These rules reflect a genuine attempt to overcome the impulse toward selectivity in private schools that might discriminate against disadvantaged students. Furthermore, the eligible schools would have to disclose enough information about themselves to permit informed consumer choices. The difficulty of forcing schools, even public schools, to release this kind of information in the past does not lead to optimism about its future efficacy. There are more than 100,000 different schools in the United States, and the voucher system could be expected to increase that number. At the very least, the interpretation and enforcement of the voucher rules will create some enormously difficult problems.[34]

The key to the regulated voucher obviously is the regulatory mechanism. The Harvard study offers alternatives but is not very precise about the problem. The report states:

> An Educational Voucher Agency (EVA) would be established to administer the vouchers. Its governing board might be elected or appointed, but in either case it should be structured so as to represent minority as well as majority interests. The EVA might be an existing local board of education, or it might be a new agency with a larger or smaller geographic jurisdiction. The EVA would receive all federal, state and local education funds for which children in the area were eligible. It would pay this money to schools only in return for vouchers.[35]

Later, the report spells out alternatives for establishing the EVA in demonstration projects:

1. The existing public school board could set itself up as the EVA.
2. The public school board could appoint a separate board as the EVA.
3. An entirely independent board including representatives of parents and staff of the participating schools could be set up.[36]

Elected or appointed, public or consortiums of participating schools, local, state, or regional? If the difference between regulated and unregulated vouchers

---

34 This provision does not mean, of course, that all schools will have the same amount of money to spend. Public schools presumably could not receive additional tax funds, but private schools could supplement their income through endowment or the support of a private organization like a church.
35 *Education Vouchers.* Center for the Study of Public Policy, *op. cit.,* p. 14.
36 *Ibid.,* p. 214.

is social justice or social disaster, then decisions about the structure of the EVA are of paramount importance.

In the demonstration projects, the principal regulator will obviously be OEO itself, but what will happen if vouchers are adopted independently by states and localities? Which of the various regulatory models—the federal agencies, state departments of education, private accrediting associations, or local school boards —leads to a reasonable belief that they could monitor this development? Which of the regulations would or could be enforced? Which would be dropped altogether? Pinning the reform of American schools on a series of ad hoc regulations to be enforced by a yet-to-be-defined EVA seems to be an enormous risk.

In reply, Jencks would insist that the current system of regulations doesn't work very well either, and EVA's wouldn't be any worse. But they might very well be worse. As I described earlier, the federal courts have become one of the principal regulators of social justice in public education. They have accomplished this by applying the First and Fourteenth Amendments to public schools. Would voucher schools involve state action and be subject to the constitutional rules the courts have established for public schools? If the answer is yes, then the ad hoc nature of Jencks' regulations and the fuzzy nature of the EVA become less dangerous, since the federal courts would continue to act as regulators. On the other hand, the concept of state action could substantially reduce the autonomy of traditionally private schools.

On this critical question the Harvard report appears to be of two minds. The two legal sections in the study are devoted primarily to discussions of the eligibility of racially segregated and parochial schools in voucher programs.[37] The authors conclude that the federal courts would prohibit the participation of any school that clearly discriminated racially, but that the participation of parochial schools awaits further court decisions. This seems to be a fair appraisal of the current state of the law. However, the report is less perceptive about the effect of state action on participating voucher schools.

In addition to being a complicated problem of law, the issue presents a tricky political situation for voucher advocates. Ninety-five percent of all private school enrollment is in parochial schools. Obviously, the support of that constituency is necessary if vouchers are to become a serious national option. Consequently, the report resuscitates the GI Bill and social security analogy to plead hopefully for the eligibility of parochial schools. But that analogy was made with unregulated vouchers and it provides a legal rationale that voucher schools do not involve state action and are thus free from constitutional restraints.[38] To concretize the

---

37 *Ibid.*, pp. 221-273.

38 Professor McCann and Miss Areen have suggested that, as long as a child chooses to attend a voucher-aided parochial school, no constitutional restrictions on the religious activity of the school would be required. Walter McCann and Judith Areen, "Vouchers

issue, could a voucher school avoid judicial standards of academic freedom or discriminate religiously in the hiring of teachers? None of the regulated voucher proposals is clear on this matter.

While not every past or future federal court decision on civil liberties and education may be the most appropriate policy for every one of the 16,000 school districts in the United States, a system of financing that runs the risk of undermining all constitutional rules in education in favor of ad hoc regulations seems to me to be too great a price to pay. Neither is it fair to private schools to be ambiguous about this point. Courts can declare that past behavior on the part of an institution requires that it meet constitutional standards from then on. In the long run, it seems doubtful that the courts would regard schools funded by tax-supported vouchers and intensively regulated by public or quasi-public EVA's as free from state action. Far better to decide that question now and to give private schools a choice. Certainly, a declaration by the responsible legislative and administrative agencies that they intended voucher schools to involve state action would constitute a proper warning and would assist courts in deciding the matter. Such a declaration would not necessarily eliminate all private schools whose current practices did not meet constitutional tests. Just as some formerly sectarian universities in New York (Fordham, for example) have altered some of their religious practices in order to receive state funds, so private schools could change to meet constitutional tests as well as ad hoc rules to become eligible for vouchers.

Vouchers as a Reform Mechanism   Even if the questions about the constitutional obligation of voucher schools were clarified, other important reservations about vouchers remain. Still, shouldn't the voucher scheme be subject to experimentation? It is difficult for any scholar or educational reformer to object to an experiment, but one may be very skeptical about whether what OEO is proposing will constitute a real experiment. In the first place, Southern cities were ruled out, although a voucher system must be workable in Columbus, Georgia, as well as Columbus, Ohio. Secondly, the experiments will take place in such few cities (only three, Seattle, Washington, Gary, Indiana, and Alum Rock, California, have applied for planning grants) that the amount of official and media attention given to these programs will eliminate the abuses vouchers might create in less scrutinized circumstances. Finally, OEO has announced that the experiments will run five to eight years,

---

and the Citizen—Some Legal Questions," *Teachers College Record*, February, 1971, p. 401. This is not a persuasive argument for two reasons. First, the Supreme Court's decision regarding religion in public schools is not based on compulsory attendance laws, but on illegal state sponsorship of religious activity. Voucher aided schools and their practices would be state sponsored under the Jencks model. Second, under a voucher system, attendance at all schools would be free and voluntary, so under their argument public schools might begin religious observations again.

but the uncertainty of program funding may cause many of the corporations and agencies otherwise interested in the educational market to hold back.

Probably a quicker, cheaper, and more accurate method of evaluating vouchers would be to test the idea through surveys. Marketing agencies do this kind of research all the time. By presenting the various voucher models to properly selected samples, reasonable forecasts could be made about what different groups of parents would do if they had vouchers. In addition, private school leaders and others who might be interested in starting schools could be surveyed to see which kind of vouchers would be acceptable to them and what kinds of new schools would be stimulated.

I suspect two findings would emerge from such a survey. First, only a tiny percentage of the traditional private or parochial schools would be willing to participate in the regulated voucher approach Jencks is proposing. Few schools would find the lottery admission feature acceptable. Entrepreneurs with the kind of organization and capital needed to offer new private educational alternatives would not find the Jencks regulations very attractive either. Some liberal, equalitarian, integration-minded parents would support the Jencks voucher model, but I suspect a much larger number of parents would opt for an unregulated, noncompensatory voucher that was free from constitutional restraints.

Those who advocate ideal or model vouchers don't seem to fully recognize the true nature of the voucher constituency. There is a latent coalition prepared to support vouchers, and it won't be led by the gentlemen scholars from Cambridge and Berkeley. The coalition is the one Kevin Phillips proposed in *The Emerging Republican Majority*.[39] It is composed mainly of Southern Protestant nativists and Northern Catholic ethnics—plus, I would add, a touch of the far right and the far left. Aid to private schools was one of the ways Phillips suggested that coalitions might be brought together. The danger is, then, that while the intellectual debate focuses on ideal vouchers, the true voucher coalition will rise up to take command of the idea. Once united, that coalition might be able to bring about the kind of unregulated, noncompensatory, constitution-free vouchers that would lead to the social disaster Jencks himself warns about.

The preceding discussion may have sounded like a plea for the status quo, but that was not its intention. Instead, I merely want to assert that the prescription for educational reform should relate more carefully to the diagnosis of the problem than do voucher proposals and that their unintended consequences may be quite damaging. As a vehicle for reform, vouchers are a very inefficient device. They would prove costly by adding to existing state and local budgets the expense of (1) all private school tuitions, (2) the EVA administrative bureaucracy, (3) new buildings and inefficient use of existing structures, (4) inefficient use of

39 Kevin Phillips. *The Emerging Republican Majority*. New Rochelle, New York: Arlington House, 1969.

existing tenured personnel, and (5) greatly increased transportation costs. Since nonparents would be partially disenfranchised from school politics by vouchers, they might be less inclined to support educational budgets, so the total financial pie would be reduced. Furthermore, to wait five to eight years for the results of the voucher experiments and then to wait until new schools are built which can provide choices is an inordinate delay of necessary educational reform. Depending on the goals chosen, there are more effective and less dangerous reform models.

If the problem is diagnosed as fundamentally one of the quality of public schools, then the experiments with performance contracting and teacher accountability should be given a chance. Each of these concepts raises difficult problems of implementation, but contains fewer risks than do vouchers. Furthermore, we might experiment with developing for the academic activities of public schools the kind of competition and rewards that already exist for extra-curricular activities.

If the problem is diagnosed as basically a problem of ideological conformity, then the spread of dual enrollment (shared time) and decentralization offers alternatives. Dual enrollment permits a student to select his curriculum from two or more learning centers. In addition to giving individuals more choice, it allows groups which have particular religious or ideological concerns to focus on those areas rather than undertaking comprehensive schooling. Many groups can find private funding for selected courses, while managing a whole school leads to public funding and public controls. Dual enrollment in some form currently exists in almost every state, and consideration should be given to the type of law recently passed in Vermont which permits the dual enrollment option in every community. The trend toward decentralizing our large city school systems is also growing. Again, a lot of problems exist, but eventually urban public schools can be expected to offer more curricular alternatives and to be more responsive to parents than before.

We can go further. In a pamphlet called "The Reform of the Urban Schools," Mario Fantini suggests a concept called "public schools of choice."[40] Fantini and his colleagues are currently writing a book on the subject and so the concept has not been fully spelled out. Essentially, however, the thesis is that we can have a lot more choices of school culture and style in urban public schools if we want them. Rather than turning to vouchers, individual choice could be promoted by developing the petition rights of parents and students. For example, a state legislature and/or local school board could establish that whenever a certain percentage of parents wanted a particular school style (British infant model, for example) or a percentage of students wanted a particular curriculum alternative,

40 Mario Fantini. *The Reform of the Public Schools.* Washington, D.C.: NEA, 1970.

public school authorities would be required by law to provide for it. If the school were set up on a house plan, as is Richard C. Lee High School in New Haven, the alternatives would exist within the same school. The only limitations would be constitutional and, in some cases, financial. Furthermore, within constitutional boundaries, there is a lot of room for experimentation with alternatives to the traditional school board as a management system.

Although these concepts are new enough to require much development, I believe they will eventually contribute more toward solving our educational problems than will vouchers. Substituting consumer accountability for political accountability is not in the long run a good bargain for either parents or society. Majority rule should be tempered with a respect for minority differences, and public education should offer many alternatives, but deciding educational policy forces a society to confront ultimate questions about its future. Such decisions are better made through the democratic process than the marketplace.

PART IV

Congressional Response

U.S. Senate

Since the Office of Economic Opportunity's voucher experiment could be funded through the agency's research budget, no specific legislation was required. Nevertheless, as the controversy over vouchers grew, committees in both Houses of Congress scheduled hearings on the proposal. The following edited exchange is between Senator Gaylord Nelson (Dem.-Wisc.) and Frank Carlucci and John Wilson of OEO.

Subcommittee on Employment, Manpower and
Poverty of the Committee on Labor and Public Welfare
Washington, D.C.
Tuesday, April 27, 1971

Senator Nelson. The subcommittee will open hearings this morning on the extension of the Economic Opportunity Act. . . .

Our first witnesses are Mr. Frank Carlucci, Director, and John Wilson, Assistant Director, Office of Economic Opportunity. The committee is pleased to have you here this morning, Gentlemen. . . .

Mr. Carlucci. Thank you very much, Mr. Chairman.

Mr. Chairman, I welcome this opportunity to appear before you today, to discuss the philosophy underlying our recent efforts in the field of education. The OEO has launched two experiments designed to find ways to improve access to a quality education for children from poor families. The first is our experiment in performance incentive contracting, which will be completed in June. The results of this experiment will be available in early fall.

The second, the regulated voucher experiment, is designed to test the effect of a financing system which places a premium on the admission of poor students and which promotes diversity in educational options for the children of the poor.

These experiments were conceived in an effort to develop innovative methods of more adequately providing students from poor families with sound schooling, and thus improving their chances of finding a productive place in American society.

I would not attempt to predict the outcome of these experiments. I do know, however, that they address in exciting new ways a problem which we can all agree is one of the primary causes of poverty—a lack of adequate education.

The experiments were designed within both the spirit and intent of the Economic Opportunity Act, which stated that OEO was developed to "mobilize the human and financial resources of the nation to combat poverty in the United States." . . .

No one doubts that an inadequate education effectively hampers an individual's chances for financial well being. I find it strange that some of our critics —or supporters, I am not always sure which—argue that OEO must be strengthened to fight the root causes of poverty, while at the same time demanding that we cease those activities designed to find better ways to educate the poor.

It is of course, comparatively easy to develop politically appealing programs that involve only spending more money and thereby supplement, rather than challenge, existing institutions.

It is much harder to examine critically basic, existing institutions, such as our educational system, that are not meeting the needs of the poor....

Mr. Wilson. . . . In my part of the testimony I would like to cover some of the specific features of the proposed experiment in educational vouchers and deal with some of the issues that have been raised with relationship to this experiment.

I would like to describe how the voucher system would operate. The parents of each child would receive a voucher which would be equal to the amount of public, local and state funds being spent in that community now.... Under the voucher system [a student] could go to a private or parochial school [as well as a public school].

Senator Nelson. If it costs more money, how would you do that?

Mr. Wilson. We are proposing that OEO would pick up the costs of students currently in parochial schools. We want to include them in the experiment if it is constitutionally possible.

So if the average public school expenditure is $800 per student, OEO would pay that amount for those private school students who want to participate and want to be included in the project.

Once the student has that voucher, say he was going to a public school now, he could go to a private school under the voucher concept.

Senator Nelson. OEO would pay the differences between the private school tuition and the per capita costs?

Mr. Wilson. No, sir. We are talking about a regulated voucher system, and we are saying that for a school to participate they cannot charge higher tuition than the basic value of the voucher.

Senator Nelson. A private school, a high school or trade school that is willing to accept a student will have to accept just the public per capita costs?

Mr. Wilson. Yes, sir.

Senator Nelson. Who is going to do that with most of those private schools in very bad trouble now? ...

Mr. Wilson. I rather doubt that the elite private schools, those charging tuition 50 or 100 percent above the average public school cost would participate. But you may have parochial schools running about the same as the low public school costs. You will have some neighborhood schools, such as in Milwaukee, where parochial schools are being closed and are being turned over to the neighborhood and are being operated as a neighborhood school and within the cost or range of feasibility.

Senator Nelson. What is the standard of eligibility? Who is eligible?

Mr. Wilson. . . . The local educational authority, which we call the educational voucher authority, which could be a reconstituted local school board determines who will be eligible to participate.

. . . The basic value of the voucher would be equal to the average expenditure. We do intend with OEO funds to supplement the value of the voucher to the poor student. There will be a compensatory payment to poor students. . . .

Students eligible would be all students attending an elementary school who would reside in the educational or the experimental area. Suppose a community such as Gary, Indiana, which has a pre-planning grant, selected 12 public schools to participate, decided they wanted to include two parochial schools. . . . They would determine the area within Gary, Indiana, and all students residing in that area would participate in the voucher experiments.

Senator Nelson. All of them?

Mr. Wilson. All of them. What they would do, instead of going automatically to the neighborhood school, they could select the elementary school to attend among those who are participating in the experiment.

The schools can only participate if, first, they are accredited and accepted and included by the local educational authority, educational voucher authority, as we call it, and meet state regulations.

Senator Nelson. So most of your schools participating would be public schools?

Mr. Wilson. Indeed, 80 percent of the total potential vacancies or positions will be provided in the public system.

Senator Nelson. What about transportation?

Mr. Wilson. We recognize that if indeed parents take advantage of this new freedom of being able to select the schools their children want to go to, there will be possibly increased costs of transportation. OEO will pick up that cost that is above the present expenditure on transportation in that system.

Senator Nelson. . . . [If you] want to go to one that is 3 miles away and there is no school bus system to get there, what do you do?

Mr. Wilson. We would have to set up a school bus system and pick up the additional cost as part of the project.

Senator Nelson. What do you visualize as the purpose of this program?

Mr. Wilson. I included in my handout a supplementary statement of tables. If you will turn to the first one, I list the primary and secondary questions we hope to answer in this experiment.

The first one is the education of poor children improved under this and second is, are parents in the community more satisfied with the educational system?

Senator Nelson. More satisfied with what educational system?

Mr. Wilson. The types of choice and flexibility and innovation we anticipate would occur under a voucher approach as opposed to the present educational system. . . .

Senator Nelson. What about people who are not poor? What is your question about them?

Mr. Wilson. We want to examine whether their education has improved also. The [main] reasons we want to undertake the experiment, however, is that . . . poor children do not have the choice of schools they can go to. Because if they are poor, and if they are black and under a neighborhood school concept they have to traditionally go to segregated schools, schools that have traditionally offered education that does not seem to meet their needs.

They do not have the money, and if they are black they cannot move into the white suburbs for better education that is offered.

What we are saying is that when you have integration, when you have more flexibility among the schools to deal with their particular problems, you will get a better educational system.

This is a hypothetical statement. It is, as a matter of fact, something we want to determine.

Mr. Carlucci. Senator, this would enable schools to specialize in certain areas and enable the parents to pick an area of particular interest, say the arts. There might be another school that specializes in technical education. . . .

Senator Nelson. You tell me these are in the elementary grades. I don't know of any great emphasis on the arts in elementary school.

Mr. Carlucci. One school might concentrate on music, for example, whereas another might concentrate heavily on math, and there are different teaching systems that might be used by different schools.

If the students and parents desired it, [a principal] could place more emphasis on a highly structured curriculum, along the lines of reading and math.

What we are saying is that we anticipate there would be interest in the system of education, the opportunity for individual principals and teachers to be more innovative in the type of curriculum they present at the elementary level.

Senator Nelson. Well, that all puzzles me. It does not seem to me it would have much impact on the school unless it involved a rather massive transfer into the system which most school systems could not take.

If it is just a few people, a hundred, who come into a primary school that has a thousand, you mean to suggest that those fifty are going to have some impact upon the curriculum of that school?

Mr. Wilson. No, the schools that will participate, the majority of the schools that will participate will be actually full voucher schools. All of the students in that school would be voucher students.

So if you have an elementary school of 500 students, they would all be there as voucher students.

Senator Nelson. Then you are saying that you have a good school, and 90 percent of the people there are from the neighborhood and would go there anyway, but they will go there now on vouchers.

Mr. Wilson. If they wanted to go to that school, they would list that as the first choice of schools they wanted to go to. Other students, if that is a good school, would also say they would want to go to the school.

We envision a lottery system, a selection system, that would be non-racial that would select the number of students that would go to that school. We anticipate that the other schools would look at the magnet school that is attracting all the students, and see what they are offering.

... Alum Rock, California, near San Jose, is one of our 3 planning areas. In that area they have a model cities school down in the poor area that has a very successful curriculum and is starting to attract parents from around who want to send their children to this school.

This is what we envision. The more flexibility you get, the greater diversity, the successful schools may attract more students.

Senator Nelson. How are you going to measure your accomplishments?

Mr. Wilson. That is difficult, because no one knows how to measure accomplishments in education now. . . .

We will use all the measures measuring the results of public education today.

That means standardized tests, it means interim performance tests, criterion reference tests. We will look at scores on the accomplishment and readiness tests, all the measures that are currently available and are being used to try to distinguish accomplishment in one school and another. . . .

Senator Nelson. How much money are you proposing to spend on the voucher system?

Mr. Carlucci. We are spending this year some 60 thousand dollars on 3 planning grants in 3 cities, Gary, Indiana; Alum Rock, California; and Seattle Washington.

We have spent $444,000 on a study of the voucher plan at the Center for the Study of Public Policy.

Senator Nelson. What do you propose to spend on the plan itself?

Mr. Carlucci. The plan itself could run possibly $5 million within the next year, going on up to maybe as high as 9 to 14 million dollars [a year] if the three cities we have indicated decide to go ahead with the experiment. . . .
We would contemplate that it would run for from 5 to 7 years. . . .

Senator Nelson. So you are talking about 70 to 100 million, somewhere in that field?

Mr. Wilson. Right.

Senator Nelson. What puzzles me, and maybe I am biased because I offered the teacher corps bill as well as the student teacher corps tutorial bill. Why not take $5 million of that and tie into the teacher corps teams and take the students in school systems and expand that program?

We are talking about getting young people involved in what is going on in America and making a contribution.

There are potentially no better tutors than high school kids themselves tutoring their peers or those who are younger. It has been done successfully time after time on individual bases. . . . But we keep coming in with experiments and experiments. We know that teacher corps concept works dramatically well.

We have had report after report after report after report from superintendents of schools, principals of schools, teachers, statistics, and everything else.

So you have got a system that is working, has been tested, that has been here suffering from lack of funds for six years or so since we got it passed, and all of a sudden we are going to try something brand new while we are starving another program which we now know works. . . .

I don't understand that. We pass programs and don't fund them and give them a chance to operate, and then we come to a brand new program.

Mr. Carlucci. There is nothing in what we are proposing, Mr. Chairman, that would prevent the teacher corps from going forward. Expenditure we think, in terms of overall expenditure, on the poor by the federal government is very modest. The kind of experiment we are proposing is designed to test what would be a more far reaching change. I think our school system has not contemplated this yet.

Senator Nelson. A far reaching change in what way?

Mr. Carlucci. By offering to poor parents the choice among schools that the wealthy presently have. We try to look at this particular experiment not with respect to education as such—we don't think we're experts in education—but we are concerned with the fact that there is a very close relationship between poverty and education, and we don't have the poor children getting the same kind of educational advantage that accrues to the children of the wealthy. . . .

Senator Nelson. Yes, but the fact is that you have got to improve the schools where the kids are. No matter how you slice it, you are not all of a sudden going to close all the poor schools in America and then transfer them someplace else to another school that is a better school than the one they were in. . . .

I would like to see everybody have the right to go wherever they please, but it ain't going to do any good just to provide a limited opportunity for a few people to do this and ignore the school that is there in the neighborhood.

Mr. Wilson. If the hypothesis for the school is correct, Mr. Chairman, we think introducing the element of competition could in itself result in improving the school that is there.

Senator Nelson. What do you mean by "competition"?

You mean the school board in a central city or Appalachia—that one of those kids is going to another school and doing better, that they are going to be embarrassed and improve their school?

Mr. Carlucci. We think if poor parents are allowed an element of choice this would induce greater responsiveness to the needs of those parents on the part of the local school system.

I would like to stress that we are not running an operating program, that this is an experiment designed to see if this kind of approach would work. . . .

Senator Nelson. . . . There are all kinds of things wrong, all kinds of rigidity in the school system, and I think the schools in the country turn children off more than they turn them on.

But transferring them around is not going to improve a school system, I don't think.

Mr. Carlucci. We are not transferring them around sir, as such. We are giving the parent a greater freedom of choice and in turn this makes the school more accountable to the parent, and if the system is indeed flexible, and this is what we are trying to determine, with the experiment, it will respond in time and there will be improvements in the kinds of education that is offered to children.

Senator Nelson. Well, you might be right.

Mr. Wilson. If you will turn to my second chart, Mr. Chairman, . . . there we list some of the changes that might occur in the schools, anticipated changes by introducing more flexibility, the opportunity for more innovation.

You see we anticipate principals and teachers will be able to determine each school's program, curriculum and area of emphasis with more flexibility than they have under the present system.

Each school will be responsible for attracting students other than on the basis of the fact that students reside in the neighborhood. Each school will operate only on the amount of funds they received from the students, and thus an ineffective school may find itself losing out financially, or have to change.

The schools in this sense will be accountable to the parents since the parents will have some degree of choice in the types of schools they go to.

Now some results from our initial pre-planning in Alum Rock say that this type of flexibility is indeed desired on the part of the teachers and the administration, where 76 percent of the teachers and 68 percent of all the administrators in that public system said there should be more alternatives to public and private schools, and only 9 percent disagreed with this. . . .

Senator Nelson. All that may be saying is that this high percentage believe, as I think they should, that people ought to have, everybody ought to have, an equal opportunity to select the best opportunity for his children that can be selected.

But you ought to have a hundred percent answer on all that. But if you are talking about this as a technique for improving the system, I guess there are a lot of better ways to do it than that.

Mr. Wilson. That we don't know at this point, Mr. Chairman.

Senator Nelson. I am talking about trying to give equal opportunity to everybody, to poor people, give them the same opportunity that well-to-do people have to select the school they want for their children, that is a good, democratic concept, fine.

But if you are talking about it as a technique for forcing a school administration that is at this stage incompetent to somehow reform itself because of the competition, I don't think that will work, because most of those don't have the capacity to reform on their own anyway. What you need is an infusion of new techniques, which is happening in the teacher corps program, and the tutorial system, that does raise the performance in the systems the children are already in.

Mr. Carlucci. This kind of system might help them to be more receptive to those techniques.

Senator Nelson. I think we ought to move to that better school as fast as we can.

Well, I am not going to argue about the experiment. I just have some questions about its accomplishing what you desire if you are talking about educational reform. If you are talking about equal opportunity for people to select the school system, that is fine, I am for that.

Mr. Wilson. If you would turn to the third chart I think in the discussions, many of the criticisms that have been made of our proposed experiment, Mr. Chairman, really reflect around the misunderstanding or the many divergent and different voucher systems that have been proposed.

Indeed, I would say there are at least four types of voucher systems that have been proposed at one time or the other in this country, or have actually been in question. One is a totally unregulated voucher system. There would be no control on the type of schools, the value of the voucher.

This is commonly referred to as the Friedman Plan in reference to Professor Friedman at the University of Chicago. It is the program that was advocated by the American Conservative Society last week.

Then you have a second approach, the segregation vouchers as I refer to it, that was attempted in the six southern states and was thrown out by the Federal courts.

Then you have a third as being discussed in several state legislatures of legislation being introduced, and it is what I call a state vouchers system. That would take the state fund that goes to public education and make that available to parents to either use in public, private or parochial schools.

Of course, the value of that voucher would be far less than the full amount of money being spent on public education now. I think the hypothesis is that if you make the voucher available you will be able to maintain parochial schools where there is a great concern they are going to close in massive numbers and send those children to public systems that cannot support it at the present time.

The fourth type of voucher system that we are talking about is a regulated voucher system. The basic areas of this in which we would regulate it are listed on chart 3. We say that no school may discriminate on the basis of race, and that all students who participate must select minority students in proportion to those minority students who apply.

All schools must be open to all applicants. The value of the voucher must be accepted as full payment, which we talked about earlier. Our only interest in including parochial schools and private schools is to have more alternatives and this is not an experiment to provide unconstitutional support to parochial schools.

If it is constitutional in the state, and then we would say within budget limitations they could participate. If it is not constitutional, then we could have a voucher without parochial schools.

We will supplement the value of the voucher to the disadvantaged students. There are two considerations for this. Some educators think it costs more to educate a poor, disadvantaged student than a bright student. That we don't know, but the value of the voucher would reflect this.

Second, if the student has a voucher that is worth more, it may be inducement to schools to be more willing to open their doors and try to appeal to that particular student.

There may be an economic incentive to the admission of the disadvantaged youth. What we are proposing is a regulated voucher system as opposed to an unregulated or a state voucher approach which are currently being discussed also.

Senator Nelson. You say that all schools must accept minority students at least in proportion to minority applicants. You realize, of course, that you will create situations where you will have an all white school, much better than that one that the blacks and Puerto Ricans or Mexican-Americans are going to. [Suppose] you have a thousand students.

Mr. Wilson. Right.

Senator Nelson. And a thousand [students] from minority groups apply, so 500 white students would have to transfer—who were going there the year before. The whites will go someplace else?

Mr. Wilson. That is true.

Senator Nelson. I want to see the first time that happens. I will discuss that with you.

(Laughter)

Mr. Wilson. We don't maintain it is going to be an easy one to launch. . . .

Senator Nelson. Well, thank you very much. We have got to get along here. We have a few more witnesses. Thank you, Gentlemen.

U.S. House of Representatives

In the House, where most educational policy
issues have been decided in recent years, the
hearings were longer and the questioning
fiercer. The following edited debate
was created when David Selden of the
American Federation of Teachers and Stanley
McFarland of the National Education
Association, who represented the
anti-voucher coalition, stated their positions
before the House Education and Labor
Committee. The Congressmen were Chairman
Carl Perkins (Dem.-Ky.), Augustus Hawkins
(Dem.-Calif.), Sam Mazzoli (Dem.-Ky.),
and William Steiger (Rep.-Wisc.). In
addition to pointing out some of the assets and
liabilities of vouchers, this dialogue indicates
how easily the voucher concept becomes
enmeshed in partisan and bureaucratic politics.

The Chairman. A quorum is present.

Our first witness is the representative of the National Education Association.

Mr. McFarland. I have with me David Selden, president of the American Federation of Teachers. The American Federation of Teachers and NEA cochair a coalition on the voucher system.

Mr. Chairman and members of this committee, we appear today as supporters of the original goals of OEO as those goals were intended by the Congress.

We are speaking for 11 organizations, with an aggregate membership of millions of Americans. These organizations are:

American Association of School Administrators
American Association of University Women
American Ethical Union
American Federation of Teachers
American Humanist Association
American Jewish Congress
American Parents Committee
Americans United for Separation of Church and State
National Association of Elementary School Principals
National Education Association
Unitarian Universalist Association

Several of the above listed organizations will testify today as to their specific objections to the voucher program. The coalition of organizations endorsing this statement is urging the committee to order the Office of Economic Opportunity to discontinue all grants for feasibility studies and funding of voucher programs at least until the Education and Labor Committee has held thorough hearings and assessed the impact of such proposals—not only on the public school system, but also on other institutions and values of American society.

It is well known by the chairman and this committee that these organizations were supporters of the original goal of the OEO—ending poverty. That is why it has been so painful for us to witness the attempt to change OEO by prematurely removing from its responsibility programs that work, eliminating programs before they have a chance to work, and becoming involved in programs that can never work—all in the name of ending poverty.

We believe that a larger issue than the voucher system is involved. The attempt of executive offices to distort, bypass, or thwart the will of Congress, not only in the withholding of appropriated funds, but also in the initiation of programs which Congress has not authorized, is becoming increasingly a matter of concern. Under the guise of research and development, such congressional mandates as the poverty program are being ignored. The original purpose of OEO—assistance to the poor—has been redirected into an ill-conceived attempt to reprivatize our social services.

We believe that programs approved by Congress should be carried out. We believe that no so-called experiments which are directly or indirectly aimed at altering or possibly destroying basic American institutions such as the public schools should be undertaken without clear direction from the Congress as representatives of the American people. . . .

Mr. Selden. Mr. Chairman, I just want to personally reinforce what Mr. McFarland has said in behalf of our coalition. We fully support the statement. Furthermore, although I don't speak for the AFL-CIO, I have been assured by representatives of the AFL-CIO that they stand in the same position.

We find particularly objectionable the use of OEO funds, which are really supposed to be used to develop economic opportunities for the poor, to promote educational experiments which have been rejected or will not be promoted by the regular educational arm of the Government. I am referring, of course, to the Office of Education. If an experiment of this kind had educational merit it certainly could have been promoted through the use of title III funds.

There is no need to go around to the backdoor and, under the guise of combating poverty, embark on an educational program which could have very far-reaching bad effects. Cancer starts with a small virus, I believe; and, while the programs that OEO is promoting in the so-called voucher system are rather small, compared to the total educational enterprise, nevertheless we fear the spread of this virus once it is allowed to take hold. . . .

Mr. McFarland. When Dr. Adron Doran, as the spokesman for NEA, appeared before this committee on April 21, 1964, we pledged the Association's support for the efforts of the Congress to eradicate poverty in this land. That pledge is still valid. We were pleased when this committee agreed with us that the Office of Economic Opportunity should not become involved in the ongoing education program of the schools, but rather should confine its activities to direct community services to the poor and to programs designed to equip poor adults to enter the world of work. Clearly, OEO was not designed to compete with the Office of Education or the established public school system.

We have watched with grave concern the destruction of the Job Corps, the downgrading of VISTA, the attempts to cut back funds for Headstart, and other similar actions. We fear that the original intent of the poverty program is being subverted from one of attack on the root causes of poverty to one which would serve as a free-wheeling research and development agency—related only very tenuously to the war on poverty.

The latest venture of this so-called research and development function of OEO is the promotion of educational voucher plans. The theory seems to be that the public school system, under the control of school boards elected by the communities they serve, is not competent to design educational programs to meet the needs of all children.

We fear that vouchers are an unconstitutional support for nonpublic schools, that they will lead to social and racial resegregation, and that they will lead to the enrichment of private sector hucksters who see this system as a bonanza.

Delegates to the 1970 NEA convention adopted the following resolution:

> The National Education Association believes that the so-called voucher plan under which education is financed by Federal or State grants to parents could lead to racial, economic, and social isolation of children and weaken or destroy the public school system.
>
> The association urges the enactment of Federal and State legislation prohibiting the establishment of such plans and calls upon its affiliates to seek from Members of Congress and State legislatures support for this legislation.

OEO has announced its intent to sink $6 to $8 million per year for the next-5 to 8 years into a so-called "voucher plan" for education. The objective is to induce local public schools to pay sums of money, equal to the school district's per-pupil cost, to parents, with the provision that the parent would select the school—public or private—which his child is to attend. The OEO planners expect the money, except for administration and transportation costs, to be contributed from local and State public school funds. The OEO planners expect the voucher stipends to be deducted from the local school district's funds. According to OEO, ... OEO "would pay the additional costs of educating students not now in the public schools." Thus, the proposal constitutes Federal aid to private schools, but not to public schools. In fact, it will reduce funds available for public education.

While the OEO plan includes what the planners consider to be adequate safeguards to prohibit racial segregation or support for religious instruction, we are fearful that such safeguards will not be characteristic of other voucher plans which will be devised in the wake of the OEO experiment. We also have strong reservations about the element of selling which nonpublic schools, especially those operated for profit, may pursue to induce parents to patronize their schools.

We are not opposed to innovation and experimentation designed to improve the quality of American education. Indeed, a major program of NEA, under its Center for the Study of Instruction, is to promote and evaluate innovative programs and to disseminate the findings of experimental research to the school systems throughout the land. But we are opposed to ventures in the guise of experimentation which are designed, despite disclaimers to the contrary, to destroy the system of public education.

We also fear that the promoters of the voucher plans in OEO have designed this as a straw to break the backs of those of us who, with the committee, hope that if we keep OEO alive long enough it would, with proper management, come again to serve its true constituency, the poor. OEO was never intended to become a sort of inhouse Rand Corp. for the systems-happy bureaucrats of any administration. We are not opposed to OEO or to continuing authorization for OEO if it is to once again be made the servant of the poor.

We fear deeply that the hidden agenda of the voucher planners is—

(1) to destroy OEO by costing it its friends, such as NEA and the other groups here today; and

(2) to create a market for the invasion of profitmaking agents who by their own admission seek to invade the social services area, not only of education but also of health. . . .

Mr. Mazzoli. . . . You mentioned in your statement, . . . Mr. Selden, that cancer starts, in your opinion, with a virus. . . . I am not a doctor, but I must accept that hypothesis. You more or less characterized the fact that probably the OEO venture in the voucher plan might lead to an erosion in the body, an erosion of public education in this country?

Mr. Selden. That is right.

Mr. Mazzoli. Do you feel this is a fair characterization of an effort to try to find a better way to try to teach our students?

Mr. Selden. The voucher plan proposes no better way or no different way to teach students. There is nothing in the plan that has any suggestion at all about methods or even goals of education. It is simply a way to channel public funds into private schools.

Mr. Mazzoli. Do you think that the Headstart program which was originally started under OEO is a good program?

Mr. Selden. Yes; and it ought to be supported. It is an example of what can be done with categorical aid. What the OEO is attempting to do in the voucher program is just the opposite. It is giving free money to anyone who can come along and grab it.

Mr. Mazzoli. Let me ask the question in this fashion. Headstart was an innovative approach in U.S. education?

Mr. Selden. Right.

Mr. Mazzoli. Headstart was the product of apparently research and development, the impetus of which was supplied by OEO. This has now been found to be a good program. Is there any possibility that a plan like vouchers could be found in the years to come to be in the very same category?

Mr. Selden. No. The chances of vouchers doing anything for education are very remote. On the other hand, the chances of vouchers doing something that could be quite harmful to education are very immediate. It is a clear and present danger. The two things are not at all comparable. . . .

Mr. Mazzoli. May I suggest this, though? Is not the voucher plan and is not performance contracting the result of citizen discontent to some extent with public education, and therefore there is an innovative approach taken, in this case, through the agency of OEO, to find out if there is a better way to train and educate our children?

Mr. McFarland. May I answer that?

This is true in performance contracting, but not in the case of the voucher plan. Mr. Glennan of the research staff of OEO indicated to us that the basic premise for the experimental so-called voucher plan was to determine whether or not poor parents could make good choices concerning where their children should go to school. Underneath it all—and I don't think this is understood by the general public—the funding that OEO proposes to contribute for the voucher plan would not go for the education of the children per se. The major funding would still come from local, State, and possibly Federal sources from the various categorical programs.

Mr. Mazzoli. Is not the voucher plan a direct result of what at least OEO people have seen in the community, a need they feel to spur on some competition maybe, to provide in competition a better kind of education for the kids who are tough to teach anyway? Is this not part of the thinking process?

Mr. Selden. Mr. Mazzoli, you ask if voucher schemes and performance contracting are not a response to public dissatisfaction with the schools. I would have to say that there is widespread dissatisfaction. We are dissatisfied with the schools, and I think Chairman Perkins is dissatisfied with the schools. I have heard him say on many occasions that we need better schools, need more money so that we can get those schools. . . .

. . . It is true; your fundamental observations are correct, that the inadequacies of our public schools today leave us open to the quacks and the people who come in with false cures.

Mr. Mazzoli. Could we characterize your testimony by saying that performance contracting plans are false cures and are quackery?

Mr. Selden. Yes, sir.

Mr. Mazzoli. Has the American Federation of Teachers or NEA themselves ever experimented with anything like performance contracting? May I ask you, have you ever experimented or thought about it?

Mr. Selden. We have studied the experiments which are now in progress.

Mr. Mazzoli. Have you studied quackery, then? If you say this is quackery, would you have suggested that that should be studied?

Mr. Selden. No. I don't think you go into things that you believe will be harmful. You might be able to cure lung cancer by stopping breathing, for instance, but I wouldn't want to try it.

Mr. Mazzoli. In other words, you do have by way of the American Federation, you do have a research and development which has gone into the problem, has it not, of performance contracting?

Mr. Selden. Investigated it, yes. . . .

Mr. Mazzoli. In the testimony this morning, basically the indication, I gather, is that performance contracting and voucher theories are not the proper province of OEO because they are designed to cure poverty and this is not their particular area. Now let me ask you, Mr. McFarland, do you think that the lack of school education is a root cause of poverty?

Mr. McFarland. Yes, I would agree with that.

Mr. Mazzoli. Is not the OEO's purpose and function to innovate, experiment, and perhaps engage in plans and programs which are designed to cure poverty?

Mr. McFarland. Yes. . . .

Mr. Mazzoli. Let me ask the following. Why should not, then, OEO get into education, if, in fact, you have stated that lack of education is a part of the root causes of poverty?

Mr. McFarland. We do not believe that the voucher system's intent or expressed purpose would achieve this at all.

Mr. Selden. Let me respond specifically. On the question of whether OEO should be in the business of educational experimentation at all, I don't think they should, because there is another branch of the Government which has that as its responsibility. So, you have OEO coming in with a program which, if it were to be carried on at all—we don't like the program in the first place—should not overlap in its intent and function the Office of Education.

We believe in strengthening the Office of Education, not diluting its function by parceling out educational projects among other governmental agencies.

Mr. McFarland. May I add something here? Really there is no voucher plan. You have the Jencks study at Harvard, you have the Friedman plan, and three or four others. It is our understanding that OEO has let several planning grants to several school systems to determine the feasibility of the voucher plan.

Mr. Mazzoli. Let me add this point. Am I correct in saying that you are as much or more opposed to voucher plans and performance contracting on the basis that they intrude upon what you believe to be the province of the Office of Education than the fact that they are quackery, as they have been characterized today?

Mr. McFarland. I would modify that slightly to say that there are many possible insidious outgrowths of the voucher plan that would be harmful to the public school system. In travels around the country and in speaking to school people who have been involved in meetings handled by OEO on education turnkey, it's evident that they were left with the impression that Federal funds would be available for the education of the children. In other words, they were led to believe that Federal research money from OEO would be available to educate the children who would be coming into the school system in addition to local and State funds. Now, I don't think this is true. I don't think this is possible.

We are raising the whole question here of whether or not, by an experimental program, an agency of the Federal Government is going to completely change the public school system. I think this is such a major question that it should be considered by itself, by this authorizing committee.

Mr. Mazzoli. Now I want to summarize, because we have other members and the Chair has been very kind to me, but I think we can summarize by saying that your objection to these two plans is much more on the basis of the theory or psychology or philosophy of this type of education than the fact that the powers and authority of Congress are eroded by the executive branch of government?

Mr. McFarland. Both, and I would make a slight distinction. My distinction is in reference to performance contracting. This is being done presently by the Office of Education.

Mr. Mazzoli. Thank you very much.

The Chairman. Mr. Steiger?

Mr. Steiger. Thank you, Mr. Chairman.

Is Christopher Jencks a quack?

Mr. Selden. I used the term "quackery." Christopher Jencks has a lot of very strong opinions I think are nonsense. It is possible that he also has some opinions that I think are very good.

Mr. Steiger. Is Dean Sizer of Harvard a quack?

Mr. Selden. Harvard did have a conference last fall. I participated in it. There were a number of people who did. You ought to get the results of that symposium. All the various proponents of the plan were there. I think you will find that those present were quite strongly—maybe 2 to 1 is a fair estimate —opposed to the voucher scheme.

Mr. Steiger. Apparently the point that Mr. McFarland has made is that there is not yet a voucher plan. Is that correct, Stan?

Mr. McFarland. Yes. We have met several times with the OEO people, including Mr. Rumsfeld when he was Director of OEO. They made it very clear that there is not a voucher plan per se. It is a very nebulous thing. When we ask specific questions about what is the intention of OEO and so forth, the response is that OEO is not promoting a voucher plan per se. They are promoting the concept. As I have indicated——

Mr. Steiger. It is very difficult for me to fully comprehend how the National Education Association can arrive at the point where it is asking Congress to prevent OEO from going ahead with something. What are you attacking, if 'it is not there yet, if it has not been tried yet? You are apparently saying that no matter what it is, or what form it is in, you don't want it.

Mr. McFarland. I am saying, because of the thrust of what we understand from OEO——

Mr. Steiger. But you are attacking something that has not even been put in a city, aren't you?

Mr. McFarland. Well, we are attacking the concept, Mr. Steiger, because we feel that it is not going to be good for the public schools.

Mr. Steiger. But you don't know that now, do you? On what basis? What proof do you have? What kind of statistics? What kind of information can you give the committee that indicates——

Mr. McFarland. I would like to turn this around and ask the question the other way. What proof does OEO have that the voucher plan might work? As I indicated earlier, the basic premise of the experimental program was not to improve education per se but to determine whether or not parents of the poor could make adequate decisions concerning where their children should go to school.

Mr. Steiger. In the hope that they might receive better education than they are receiving now. I trust the chairman will allow OEO to come here to explain the voucher plan, which at this point he has not been able to do. You are here in an advocacy position telling the Congress that it does not make any difference what it is, you don't like it, period. You don't want OEO to be able, under the law, to undertake this experiment, if I understand your statement correctly.

Mr. McFarland. Mr. Steiger, if you will refer to the latter part of the statement, we are asking this committee or the Congress to take a very hard look at this before the experimentation continues.

Mr. Steiger. I see. You want to prejudge the experiment? Your posture is one of saying that you don't want to see the results of the experiment. You just don't want the experiment to go on?

Mr. McFarland. We are suggesting that OEO should present their experiment to this committee for their consideration.

Mr. Steiger. Should we have said that with Headstart? You talk about OEO, "invading the field of education." Was Headstart an invasion of the field of education? Do either of you think that?

Mr. McFarland. No.

Mr. Steiger. Does the AFT think that was an invasion of the field of education?

Mr. Selden. Rather than going through a cross-examination I would like to explain the question——

Mr. Steiger. I would appreciate your responding as to whether or not you agree with the NEA position that OEO invaded the field of education.

Mr. Selden. Certainly; we support that completely.

Mr. Steiger. You support Headstart?

Mr. Selden. Yes, we do. And we wish Headstart had been carried on by the Office of Education. It should be transferred to the Office of Education.

Mr. McFarland. It is in HEW now. It has been transferred to the Office of Child Development.

Mr. Steiger. It started on OEO.

Mr. Selden. It was not an experiment, however.

Mr. Steiger. It was not?

Mr. Selden. Everyone knew that the children of the poor needed a headstart to get along in school. It did not take any experimentation to determine that this was a good idea. The problem was to get the money to do it. The public school system certainly did not have the funds to carry on this kind of program. They don't to this day. Therefore, when Headstart was set up with OEO funds, it was welcomed because this was a way of putting some additional money into the school system, in effect.

Mr. Steiger. Wait a minute; you just got through saying it was a way of putting more money into the school system. You know that is not right. With all due respect to the AFT, you have a host of different kinds of Headstart programs: some run by churches, some run by universities, some run by school systems.

Mr. Selden. I thought you were referring to OEO Headstart.

Mr. Steiger. That is not a way of putting more money into the school system.

Mr. Selden. Into education.

Mr. Steiger. And experimenting with new ways of delivering educational services to the children?

Mr. Selden. Not at all. It was not an experiment in that sense at all. One of the problems with performance contracting as well as vouchers, incidentally, is that initially they are using additional funds. For instance, there is a performance contract run by Singer-Graflex and financed by OEO in Seattle. I have visited it and looked at it. It seems a good program. It is based, though, on the idea of providing an additional $237 worth of services per child for the children who are underachieving in school; young kids.

Nothing can be wrong with that. I don't care how ineffective the program is. It is an additional effort being made on those children. One should evaluate, though, if you want to make an appropriate judgment, as to whether or not that $237 might have been spent better in some other way rather than by giving it to Singer-Graflex and the people running that particular project.

Now, to get back to your original question of the voucher plan. Mr. McFarland is quite right in that there is no precise voucher plan but there is a voucher idea, a voucher concept. If I get your approach to this, Mr. Steiger, it is sort of like buying the "thing"; that we ought to put up the money to buy the "thing" and then we will see whether the "thing" is good for schools.

Mr. Steiger. On the contrary. I am not buying anything. I don't know whether vouchers are good or bad.

Mr. Selden. Then, you ought not to give money for a thing called vouchers. That is the point.

Mr. Steiger. Beautiful. Thank you. That is as clear an explanation as I have heard yet. I am amazed at the conservatism——

Mr. Selden. We never claimed to be radical.

Mr. Steiger (continuing). Of the two national education associations. It bothers me, I must admit. I am disturbed by this stick-your-head-in-the-sand kind of attitude that you are exhibiting here this morning. I say that with deep respect for the organizations that you represent. But I cannot for the life of me understand how you can deny to OEO an opportunity to experiment. We should not have gone ahead with Job Corps, apparently.

Mr. Selden. That is debatable.

Mr. Steiger. Does Mr. McFarland agree with me that OEO should not have gone ahead with Job Corps?

Mr. McFarland. That is why we are here. Mr. Steiger. We feel this issue is so important that this voucher concept should be considered by this committee before an agency of the Federal Government, OEO, proceeds with the experiment. We are raising with this committee the fears, the concerns that we have, and we are asking you to take a look at this and to judge it.

Mr. Steiger. But you are asking us not to judge it; you are asking us to cut it off.

Mr. McFarland. That is right. We are expressing our concerns. That is our input to you. I am sure OEO will come in when they have an opportunity to testify and take the other position.

Mr. Steiger. I am trying to find out why you want us to cut it off. Frankly, you have not answered that.

Mr. McFarland. To me, basically the voucher plan is an alternate way of financing nonpublic schools. The funding situation at the local and State level is critical. Federal support of public education has proportionately decreased in the last several years. For the life of me, I do not understand how a public school district can split up the pie, the present financial pie, to educate these additional children on the basis of an experiment designed to determine whether or not poor parents can make an adequate judgment as to where their children should go to school.

Mr. Steiger. We agree, do we not, that there are serious problems with the education that is now available for disadvantaged children across the country? That is fair, is it not?

Mr. McFarland. Yes.

Mr. Steiger. AFT would agree with that, would they not?

Mr. Selden. We have stated this many, many times, and you are familar with our publications. I wrote a column just last month pointing out that big city elementary schools may be the epicenter of an educational earthquake.

Mr. Steiger. Then we have agreed that there are serious problems. Would we also, then, agree that one has to give some consideration to alternative education?

Mr. Selden. Not necessarily at all. I think you look at these schools and you see what is wrong with them and you give them the money to improve themselves. You don't try a whole new approach.

Mr. Steiger. What if we said—well, we can think of a million and one types of different alternatives that might be available. It concerns me a little bit that you are not willing to give consideration to something else. . . .

The Chairman. I was conducting that hearing in 1964 when we set up this poverty program. I invited Dr. Doran, who was the representative before the committee at the time representing the NEA. It was the purpose of the Office of Economic Opportunity to be the spokesman for the poor people throughout this land, but for the last 2 years the philosophy has changed.

We commenced to spin off all of these programs that the old line departments never would take any action on or do anything for the poor. Now we are passing them back to the old line agencies and seeing the function of the Office of Economic Opportunity as an innovation, research, and letting it go at that. That never was the real function of the Office of Economic Opportunity, if you go back to 1964 when we set this thing up or in later years.

So naturally we all want to innovate and do everything possible. I am saying that we should be doing so much more for the poor, for the poor children, preschool children, through the Office of Economic Opportunity—for Headstart, all types of children where we are not puttting money. But it has been generally recognized for 175 years that we cannot maintain two school systems, a private school system and a public school system. That has been recognized for 150 or 175 years and adhered to by the courts.

But notwithstanding here we come with an experiment that the OEO is going to have the opportunity to explain. But the question that remains in my mind here this morning, if you added the money that they are giving away in this voucher plan to the public school system, is there any evidence anywhere along the line that the good would not inure to that public school system if the money was given to those children in the public school system?

Mr. Steiger. Mr. Chairman, that same argument might be used that we ought to have given the $200 million that was available to the Job Corps to the public school system that obviously had failed the Job Corps graduates.

The Chairman. Not at all.

Mr. Steiger. I think that is exactly the same thing. What would have happened if we had given the Headstart money?

The Chairman. Why don't we give it to the poor in the area of preschool where we don't get in a religious controversy? That is where we should be giving these funds in preschool. Instead of getting something out here and getting a controversy started, where to say the least there is no proof of success anywhere along the line.

Mr. Steiger. But there is not proof of failure either. This is the whole point.

The Chairman. I am saying wait until we get all the facts in.

Mr. Steiger. The two witnesses this morning are telling us, don't worry about the facts, we don't care what it looks like, we oppose it, period.

The Chairman. We are going to get the facts, notwithstanding any witness.

Mr. Steiger. But it is a little difficult to get the fact when the experiment has not even been tried yet.

The Chairman. We are going to get the facts. . . .

Mr. Steiger. Let me return to what I began to say before the chairman made this comment.

On page 3, you say:

> There is a hidden agenda of voucher planners. One is to destroy OEO by costing it its friends, such as NEA and other groups here today, and then secondly to create a market for the invasion of profitmaking agents who, by their own admission, seek to invade the social service area not only of education, but also of health.

Would you expand on that? What are you talking about? . . .

Mr. McFarland. We have serious questions about its relationship to the elected school boards. The Jencks plan, for example, talks about setting up a voucher agency that would train and give information to parents to assist them in making adequate decisions as to what schools their children should attend. It is unclear in any proposal as to really what the relationship would be between these ad hoc groups and the elected representatives, the school boards in this case.

Mr. Steiger. Let me go back to the point I have tried to make. No one can argue with raising questions, but the questions you raise, it seems to me, none of us can answer now, rightly or wrongly.

Mr. McFarland. We have raised them with OEO and we have not been able to get any satisfactory answers. I was hoping you might be able to get some answers by raising the questions here. . . .

Mr. Steiger. Could either of you comment on one suggestion which has been raised about vouchers, that is, de facto residential segregation is an important problem with which we have to come to grips, and one of the underlying concepts of voucherism is to make possible the transferability of pupils between schools; is that a better idea, let us say, than busing as it is now done?

Mr. Selden. I personally feel that our school systems, our school districts as set up, are probably unconstitutional because they do foster racial segregation. But I want to point out that we have a great deal of experience with voluntary busing. I am not criticizing what is being done in the South. We are supportive of this and think it should be extended to northern cities.

But in the early days of integration, after the 1954 Supreme Court decision, there were many northern school systems that put voluntary open enrollment plans into effect. That is, children would be bused free of charge out of their slum ghetto environments and allowed to attend schools on a space-available basis in the middle-class areas of the school district involved. Almost none of those open-enrollment programs are still in operation.

In the first place, there wasn't space available for many of the children who wanted to transfer out, and I think you will find that there wouldn't be spaces available in the suburbs, either, for slum children that have vouchers in their hands.

The other reason is, that the busing was all one way and it was not compulsory. It was a great deal of effort for young children to ride that bus a long distance to another school. It was an effort for the parents of the child to confer with the teachers about how the child was doing. The open enrollment plans have failed.

Mr. McFarland. Mr. Steiger, I am glad you raised that question, because that is one of our questions. This could work in reverse. In other words, the voucher plan would not assist in integration. . . .

Mr. Steiger. I might just say, Mr. Chairman, that I have listened today and have read the testimony in an effort to better understand this strange kind of opposition that exists to that experimentation being undertaken by OEO. I make no bones about whether a good result or bad result will come from the concept or the specific plan for vouchers or performance contracting.

None of us know that. You don't know and we don't know it. To raise question is fine, but I simply say to you in all honesty that to come out, as you have done, in opposition to even undertaking it leaves me absolutely cold.

Mr. Mazzoli. I must say, Mr. Chairman, that I have to agree with him. That was my major problem this morning, the very fact that such clear lines of total opposition were drawn by the two gentlemen without really having any knowledge on their part as to whether or not these two plans will work.

Likewise, OEO has no experimental results to show whether the plans will work. They are simply proposing this, and we are trying to find out should they continue in their experimental efforts.

I share the gentleman from Wisconsin's concern and puzzlement over the fact that there is fairly such strong opposition without having the things followed through. . . .

The Chairman. Mr. Hawkins.

Mr. Hawkins. Mr. Chairman, I disagree with the gentleman. It seems to me that the witnesses are really not opposing experimentation, but they are really opposing experimentation with the poor. It seems to me that this is the worst possible abuse of money. If you are going to experiment, don't take it away from the poor people. . . .

The Chairman. This is the same philosophy which has been going on over the past 2 years, just gradually destroying the Office of Economic Opportunity under the pretense of trying to fool the public that they are doing something for the poor. . . .

Mr. Steiger. I have to disagree with both of you. If you want to argue about the merits of vouchers and performance contracting, do that. But I don't think you can take that argument into the concept of the destruction of OEO. The research and development part of OEO has been in existence since 1965 when the act was passed. You know this is something entirely different from the concept of trying to destroy the agency.

Mr. Hawkins. I don't think it is. What we are trying to indicate is that, as you use more and more of the money which is limited and which is being certainly cut back, as you use that money for different experimental purposes you obviously will take it away from other much needed programs.

No one disagrees that some experimentation is valid and it should be certainly fostered and this we do not disagree with you on.

But the point is, why take a very limited amount, for example, the President's Council on Youth Opportunity has been disbanded at a time when it is badly needed. There is now not a single coordinating agency to take care of a problem that we know is going to develop this summer. Now, certainly some money could be used for that. VISTA is being disbanded. One by one, all of the programs are being disbanded, dismantled, reorganized, merged. Whatever, you want to call it, it simply means that the administration is not willing to face the fact that they are destroying the Office of Economic Opportunity and they don't want to say that.

So, they use rhetoric, strange language—we are going to experiment with something. And gradually the entire program is being washed out. Now, the poor are going to wake up a few months from now and they are not going to have a program. The local officials will be looking for some of this revenue-sharing money and they are not going to have any assistance. The whole thing is going to be geared to a complete fiasco.

I am surprised at the response that the Congressman, a very able and progressive Congressman from Wisconsin, would not want to protect at least a program that offers a little help.

Mr. Steiger. I am trying to protect it against those who are trying to destroy it.

Mr. Hawkins. I think you are looking the wrong way for the enemy, then. Seriously speaking, what do you expect in the way of a program this session, if this committee is going to be left with a title to pass to be continued 2 years and all the programs are going to be transferred out of the Office of Economic Opportunity? Who is going to coordinate the economic opportunity program?

Mr. Mazzoli. I believe, Mr. Hawkins, the gentleman said one of their main objections to this was that the programs would remain in OEO, interestingly enough. If it is going to be done, they want to shift it to the Office of Education and not stay in OEO.

Mr. Selden. You are misrepresenting my position on this.

Mr. Mazzoli. I thought one of the main objections here was the fact that experimental education programs should be done under OE and not OEO.

Mr. McFarland. Conducted in the regular public school systems, K through 12.

Mr. Selden. In the first place, I am opposed, my organization is opposed to vouchers and performance contracting as a matter of principle. We don't want them transferred any place except out.

Just a minute! I have a right—maybe I don't have any right here, I don't know—anyway, we think that OEO got into the education business by the back door and is promoting educational experiments which really, if they were to be done at all, ought to be done through the regular educational arm of the Government, the Office of Education.

But we do have specific objections to both of these proposals and we think that this is what happens when you have people who really don't understand anything about education coming along and putting some money into it.

Mr. Mazzoli. In other words, if the money is going to be used, OEO should not use it; it should be done by the Office of Education?

Mr. Seldon. I feel that clarifies my statement.

Mr. Mazzoli. I yield back to Mr. Hawkins.

Mr. Hawkins. I don't think that there is anything new to this idea of the private system operating schools. It preceded the public school system, itself. It was largely confined to the elite. There is nothing strange about companies operating programs of this nature. I would doubt to some extent whether experimentation is needed, but I am willing to stipulate that if we are going to have experimentation, then, give somebody else the money to play around with and don't take it out of the mouths of the poor.

That is the only point I am making. Other than that, if you want to experiment, let the administration come up with some money. Apparently it can find it some place, and give its bureaucrats, some political appointees, the money to go out and experiment with it, if that is what it wants to do. But don't, under the guise of trying to do something for the poor, take money away from them and waste it on this type of experimentation. . . .

The Chairman. Thank you very much, gentlemen. I think it is very appropriate that these questions be raised at this time. It will be most helpful in the consideration of the various programs and evaluating the various programs by the committee, that these questions be raised so that we can consider them fairly.

Mr. McFarland. Thank you very much.